IN MEMORY OF:

Mrs. Doris Ayres

PRESENTED BY:

Mr. & Mrs. Michael Roseberry

# Cheesecake

## COOKBOOK

# Cheesecake

## COOKBOOK

50 To-Die-For Recipes for New York–Style Cheesecake

**ALAN ROSEN & BETH ALLEN**

PHOTOGRAPHY BY MARK FERRI

The Taunton Press

*In tribute to our loyal, devoted, hardworking staff and family members
who make Junior's restaurants great places to enjoy family and friends
—and, of course, a slice of the world's most fabulous cheesecake.*

The Taunton Press, Inc., 63 South Main Street, PO Box 5506, Newtown, CT 06470-5506
e-mail: tp@taunton.com

Editor: Pamela Hoenig
Jacket/Cover design: Carol Singer
Interior design: Carol Singer
Layout: Carol Petro
Photographers: Mark Ferri (interior and cover); photo on p. ii by Zach DeSart
Food stylist: AJ Battifarano
Prop stylist: Francine Matalon-Degni

LIBRARY OF CONGRESS CATALOGING-IN-PUBLICATION DATA
Rosen, Alan, 1969-
 Junior's cheesecake cookbook : 50 to-die-for recipes for New York-style cheesecake / Alan Rosen & Beth Allen.
    p. cm.
 Includes bibliographical references and index.
 ISBN-13: 978-1-56158-880-0 (alk. paper)
 ISBN-10: 1-56158-880-6 (alk. paper)
 1. Cheesecake (Cookery) 2. Cookery--New York (State)--New York. I. Allen, Beth. II. Title.

TX773.R785 2007
641.8'653--dc22

                          2007001788

Printed in the United States of America
10 9 8 7 6 5 4 3

*About the recipes in this book:* These recipes have been adapted in the Junior's style, in small quantities for preparation in home
kitchens. Many of these cheesecakes are baked regularly at Junior's and are available in Junior's restaurants, by mail order, and/or on
the Internet at www.juniorscheesecake.com. Others have been created in the Junior's style especially for this book. Junior's does not
use gelatin in their cooking, but a certified kosher stabilizer instead. However for easy and reliable home preparation, a few of these
recipes use gelatin. If this is a concern for you, ask your local kosher grocer for a gelatin replacement.

# Acknowledgments

*My sincere thanks to…*

• Junior's—the restaurant, the Rosens, their skilled and very welcoming staff, and the makers of the world's most fabulous cheesecake. Without them, this book could never have happened. And because of them, New Yorkers, visitors, and folks worldwide can enjoy cheesecake at its New York best.

• Alan Rosen, my co-author, who loves to share his passion for cheesecakes—the way to mix the batter, the slow way to bake the cakes, the gentle way to cool them, and, of course, the perfect way to slice them. Over many delicious slices of cheesecake and cups of coffee with Alan, his brother Kevin, and his father, Walter, I have come to treasure the story of the Rosens—their family memories and traditions, their profound food knowledge, and, most of all, their commitment to "the best" in all they do. The Rosens and their highly capable staff have an inherent ability to make every customer feel they are very special—the moment he or she walks into one of Junior's New York restaurants, or takes a bite of a Junior's cheesecake that has been hand-delivered to home.

• Michael Goodman, master baker extraordinaire, who always found time to show me how they carefully bake or finish a particular cheesecake or quickly shower a cake with chocolate ganache. He let me experience firsthand the day-to-day happenings in the bakery—the professional skill of the bakers, their careful attention to every cake, and their conscientious attention that makes each cake perfect.

• Nancy Weinberger—the marketing whiz who is helping the Rosens continue to grow the business, especially through mail order, Internet, and wholesale channels. She always found the time to help me locate a recipe, research a cheesecake fact, or find a freshly baked cake for me to taste.

• Pam Hoenig—executive editor at the Taunton Press, who has known and believed in the Junior's story for years and was instrumental in visualizing this beautiful book of cheesecakes, made the Junior's way. She was always as close as my computer and my telephone, ready to help edit a recipe, solve a baking issue, select the fifty perfect cheesecakes, and somehow always found time to add her expert baking knowledge and advice along the way.

• And the rest of the Taunton Team—Without any doubt, it took the top professional group at Taunton Press to turn the manuscript into this lovely keepsake: assistant editor Katie Benoit, who efficiently moved everything along to production; Carol Singer, for her artistic book design; editorial production manager Kathleen Williams; art director Chris Thompson; photo editor Wendi Mijal; marketing director Melissa Possick; publicity maven Pamela Duevel; sales director Kevin Hamric; and publisher Jim Childs.

• The Photography Team—The gorgeous photographs scattered among these pages required a top group highly skilled in photographing food, especially cheesecakes: photographer Mark Ferri and his assistant Mark Jordan; food stylist AJ Battifarano and her assistant Amy Marcus; and prop stylist Francine Matalon-Degni.

• The Public Relations Team—Getting the word out about this book to you, the reader, takes a highly qualified team of public relations professionals. Many thanks go to executive vice president Bruce Bobbins and account executive Wallis Post from the Dan Klores Communications agency and food publicist Carrie Bachman.

• To all who know, love, and enjoy Junior's cheesecakes—from the "regulars" who drop by frequently for a slice of cake and a cup of coffee, to neighbors, celebrities, journalists, presidents, politicians, mail-order recipients, famous visitors, not-so-famous folks, experienced bakers and those are ready to bake and taste a fabulous Junior's cheesecake for the very first time. Each of you makes the countless hours of recipe testing and tasting well worth every delicious bite.

—Beth Allen

# Contents

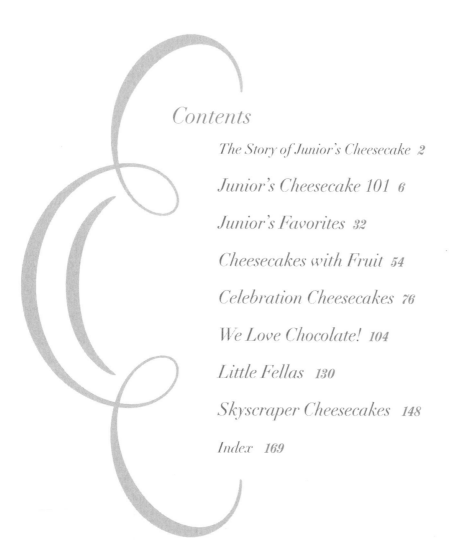

# The Story of
## Junior's Cheesecake

*Welcome to Junior's*, the home of the #1 New York cheesecake, the cheesecake that all others aspire to be. Come on down to Brooklyn, to the corner of DeKalb and Flatbush Avenue Extension, and find out what makes this cheesecake better than any other. You'll feel right at home the minute you open the door—someone's always there, smiling and waiting to say, "Welcome to Junior's!" Take a seat at the counter and order a slice of our famous cheesecake, just like folks have been doing ever since the 1950s. Now get ready for the best cheesecake you've ever tasted!

At first glance, you'll see that Junior's cheesecake is different from all the others. This slice of cheesecake is straightforward, plain, and homemade looking. Nothing fancy, not even sour cream or whipped cream on top. Rather, it's cake-like and golden on top, not pale or milky white. And no graham cracker crust for this cake! Instead, it's baked on a delicate sponge cake—the same kind you make for a birthday cake. Put in your fork to break off a bite. It's so dense and rich that it holds together and still stands proud—not dry or crumbly. Now, take a taste. It's smooth, satiny, oh-so-creamy, and so good that you're immediately ready to take a second bite—then another and another until only the memory of the best cheesecake you've ever eaten is left. As the reporter Ron Rosenbaum once wrote in *The Village Voice*, "The cheesecake at Junior's is like 'edible ivory.' It's the closest thing to heaven one can imagine—it's a slice of cheesecake, made the real New York way."

As you might expect, a cake this fine wasn't created in a day!

### It All Began on Cherry Street
It was 1904, the year Grandpa Harry was born to his parents, Sarah and Barnett Rosen, who had emigrated a few years before from the Ukraine. They were very poor and lived in a tenement on Cherry Street on the Lower East Side of Manhattan. They had six children; Grandpa Harry (Hershel) was the second oldest of their four sons. Barnett worked twelve hours a day at the Wilson & Company's slaughterhouse.

Sarah was ten years younger than her husband. Though she was illiterate, she was energetic, wise, skillful, and resourceful. The Rosens were masters at making the best of what they had. To help bring in money, Sarah ran a small newsstand. One day, when she was fifty-one, she was gathering some ice that had fallen off an ice wagon. She was pinned beneath the heavy wagon wheels and her arm was so badly hurt that it had to be amputated. But she continued to work to make some money. All along, Sarah and Barnett squirreled away everything they could.

My great-grandmother Sarah was probably the single source that drove her sons, my Grandpa Harry and his older brother Mike, to success. She saw to it that they always worked every day after school, not far from home, at Marchioni's Ice Cream Parlor. Sarah would give them fifty cents a week of the money they had earned to frivolously spend any way they wished, then she saved every penny of their earnings over that. In just two years she had $1,500, so she bought them a partnership in a luncheonette on Duane Street and Broadway. Grandpa was only sixteen and his brother Mike, eighteen. They soon became known for some of the best sandwiches and sodas around. They bought out their partner, and expanded to shop after shop, until they had their own chain in Manhattan called the Enduro Sandwich Shops.

In 1928, Grandpa took his bride-to-be, Ruth Jacobson, to the corner of DeKalb and Flatbush Avenue Extension in Brooklyn, the same corner where Junior's stands today. "Right here is where we will open the next Enduro Sandwich Shop," he told her proudly. Ruth, a twenty-year-old from the Bronx, knew only that Brooklyn was infamous for gangsters, bootleg breweries, and waterfront dives. "Harry, what are you thinking? This place is a morgue." Grandpa looked at her with a smile she soon learned expressed his love of challenge and confidence. "If I listen to you, my darling, we'll be wearing cigar boxes for shoes."

## Corned Beef on Rye, Please

In February 1929, Grandpa and his brother Mike opened the shop in the Brooklyn location. Business was good, but then the stock market crashed and they lost a lot of money. They ended up selling most of their Enduro shops in Manhattan, and concentrated all of their efforts on the Enduro in Brooklyn. When Prohibition was repealed, Grandpa and his brother expanded again, this time adding a cocktail bar and an elevated bandstand, turning his luncheonette into a full-scale Enduro Restaurant and Café. By then, he had two sons—my uncle, Marvin, and my dad, Walter. From 1934 to 1949, the Enduro was *the* place to dine, drink, and dance. But by 1949, the servicemen were gone and the general public stopped flocking to the Enduro steakhouse with its glitzy nightclub look. It fell deep in debt and eventually closed. Mike wanted to call it quits and eventually did, but Grandpa still had his dreams and his vision.

## Sprinkle a Little Sugar

Grandpa was full of ideas on how to salvage the business. He saw a family dining place for the future, a safe and reassuring place that served good homemade food and lots of it. It would be modern and sleek: bright orange Naugahyde® booths, light wooden counters, and futuristic hanging lamps. We still have that same look today. Grandpa needed a new name, so he chose Junior's, in honor of his two sons, Marvin and my dad, Walter.

Grandpa often said, "Sprinkle a little sugar on the table, and the ants will come." And he was right. Junior's opened on Election Day in 1950. Red, white, and blue banners flew in the breeze, sweet bakery aromas drew in the customers, and Grandpa gave them what they wanted—excellent home-cooked food, impeccable service, the best desserts anywhere, and, most of all, his welcoming smile. So the folks came, from early morning until the wee hours of the night. And they kept on ordering: thick juicy hamburgers, fresh brisket on challah, creamy egg salad, mile-high malteds, and sundaes smothered with hot fudge and topped with whipped cream. They loved it all and they kept coming back day after day.

Grandpa knew if he was going to have a great restaurant in New York, he had to offer the best baked goods around, so he hired the Danish baker Eigel Peterson. The pair soon became a familiar sight in the bakery, working alongside each other all hours of the day. Almost everywhere Grandpa went, he brought back some baked goods that he liked: a sweet bread one day, a slice of a three-layer devil's food cake the next, a piece of berry pie another day. Then he and Eigel would spend hours in the bakery trying to make them. They would bake and taste, then bake some more, until they came up with something even better looking and tasting, and good enough to put on the menu. Some are still on the menu today: fresh strawberry shortcake (four layers!), cherry crumb pie, apple strudel, and the creamiest rice pudding you've ever tasted.

## Creating Cheesecake the Junior's Way

Grandpa also knew that a great New York restaurant had to have a great cheesecake. So he set out to make the best cheesecake in the world. He started bringing in samples from the places known for their cheesecakes: Lindy's, Reuben's, the Brass Rail, even the local diner down the street. He and Eigel would taste each one, then they would start baking. The crust of one cake was just right but the cheese filling was too dry and crumbly. The creaminess of another was perfect but its graham cracker crust didn't work. Still another had that melt-in-your-mouth creaminess but lacked a subtle, sweet flavor.

Finally, they thought they had found the magical formula and their customers agreed. They kept hearing that Junior's cheesecake simply tasted better than any cheesecake they had ever put into their mouths. Whatever it was,

they had done it; they had finally created the Junior's way to make cheesecake!

The customers kept coming and they kept ordering slices of Junior's New York cheesecake: Elvis Presley, John Lindsay, Bobby Kennedy, Abe Beame, Ed Koch, Reverend Al Sharpton, Joe Torre, Robert DeNiro, and regular Brooklynites from all walks of life. My dad, Walter, and my uncle Marvin became regulars too, as they became more and more active in running Junior's.

## We're Number 1!

On July 26, 1973, writer Ron Rosenbaum published his column in *The Village Voice* challenging anyone anywhere to find a better cheesecake than the one baked at Junior's. "There will never be a better cheesecake than the cheesecake they serve on Flatbush Avenue. . . . "

Then during the fall of 1973, a panel of six experts from *New York* magazine set out to find the best cheesecake in New York. Our cake was one of twelve New York–style plain cheesecakes they brought back to their office to judge. As the story goes, they rated each one for freshness, the quality of ingredients, and just plain good taste. Finally they found the winner: all six judges unanimously chose Junior's cheesecake the Champion Cheesecake of all cheesecakes in New York City. We even beat out the cakes from the famous Stage Deli and Ratner's. Though we didn't realize it at the time, we were well on our way to becoming famous!

After the magazine hit the stands, the news traveled fast, well beyond Brooklyn. More and more folks came to Junior's—each one wanting a big slice of our cheesecake. Our business grew quickly; on an average day, we served about 500 slices and packed another 500 cheesecakes to go. Our staff baked around the clock to keep up with the demand. By 1977, Junior's was producing 5,000 cheesecakes every week!

## Save the Cheesecake!

But it hasn't all been roses for us. Late one hot August Sunday night in 1981, a three-alarm fire broke out at Junior's. Luckily, all fifty of our employees and seventy-five customers got out safely. The firemen worked for 2½ hours putting out the fire. At the end of that long night, there was little left but ashes where Junior's had stood. While the firefighters worked through the night, we all came. Folks from the neighborhood were there too, chanting: "Save the cheesecake, save the cheesecake!"

We started cleaning up right away. Our staff, from bakers to cooks to waiters, was there, even though they knew they would be out of work for months. We all pitched in to save the cheesecake. We began almost immediately baking our cakes in some spare oven space in the old Barton Candy factory on DeKalb. We sold them as fast as we could bake them at our Cheese Cakerie, which we opened in the Albee Square Mall nearby.

In less than a year, on May 27, 1982, Junior's reopened on the same corner. It had that same Junior's look, but now we were bigger and better. We now had room to seat 450 instead of 350, plenty of extra space for parties, a fully stocked bar, and even a sidewalk café. We updated all of our kitchens and added a refurbished bakery. Dignitaries came and declared it Junior's Day in Brooklyn. Customers came from near and far; they lined up from early in the morning until late at night for a slice of our cheesecake. No one seemed to mind waiting. It was just liked Grandpa always said: "Give folks what they want, when they want it. If you do that, they will come." And they did. They would wait for hours for a slice of Junior's cheesecake.

## Junior's: The Most Fabulous Cheesecake in the World

Brooklyn began renovating in the 1980s and continued through the '90s and right on into the next century. More and more families started staying or returning to Brooklyn and young professionals came too, to get away from the high rents in Manhattan. Junior's has continued to grow along with the neighborhood, expanding in ways even we never dreamed possible.

I made my first appearance on the QVC℠ TV Shopping Network in the fall of 1995. Before my show was over, the phones started ringing. We sold 2,400 cheesecakes in 4½ minutes. Even for Junior's, that's a lot of cakes! And we had only ten days to deliver. Our ovens were going twenty-four hours a day. Soon, my appearances were producing 27,000 orders, so we hired more bakers and started baking more cheesecakes.

The rest is history. Junior's has now become the authority on cheesecakes—especially New York cheesecake. Writer Raymond Seitz summed it all up in an article in the *Conde Nast Traveler*: "Few things in life are certain. But one incontestable verity is that Junior's serves the best damn cheesecake in New York, or as its proprietors, the Rosen family, might say with typical Brooklyn dissidence, 'the most fabulous cheesecake in the world.' "

You can still enjoy a slice of cheesecake at our flagship restaurant in Brooklyn. But if you can't visit us there, stop by our Junior's restaurant and bakery in Grand Central Station in midtown Manhattan. Or drop by our newest home in Shubert Alley in Times Square. If you're not near New York City, just pick up the phone and we'll ship a cheesecake right to you, the very next day, wherever you live.

Over the years, our bakers have baked over a hundred different varieties of Junior's cheesecakes, from our famous plain original New York cheesecake to some traditional favorites of chocolate mousse, strawberry swirl, and cherry crumb. Our newest creations are towering skyscraper cakes—actually a cake-within-a cake, such as Fresh Strawberry Shortcake Cheesecake and Carrot Cake Cheesecake. Whichever one you want, you'll find it at Junior's! And now, thanks to this book, you can bake cheesecake at home in your own kitchen, the famous Junior's way.

Enjoy!

—*Alan Rosen*

# Junior's Cheesecake 101

*Ever since the 1950s,* the bakers at Junior's have been making cheesecakes twenty-four hours a day. Over the years, they've perfected it all: the type of pan to use, the best technique for mixing the batter, and the best way to bake the cake (always in a water bath). And once they've taken the cake out of the oven, they've discovered how to let it cool, how long to chill it, and which knife to use to cut it so each slice stands up straight, looking light, creamy, and homemade. The recipes are all perfected, too. Whichever flavor they're baking, each one is based on the same original cheesecake recipe, created in the 1950s by Grandpa Harry Rosen. It simply tastes better than any other cheesecake you've ever tasted!

Many of the tips and techniques in this chapter and scattered throughout the pages of this book have been shared by the Rosens, especially Alan Rosen. I also gathered many techniques for making cheesecakes the Junior's way while baking alongside the professional bakers at Junior's flagship bakery in Brooklyn and during many sessions at Junior's specialty cake bakery with Master Baker Michael Goodman. I adapted the recipes to make one cake at a time, instead of fifty or a hundred, and revised the directions to use home equipment, mixers, and ovens, similar to the ones you have in your own kitchen. Now it's all here, for you to read, use, and refer to often.

Whether you're already an accomplished baker or picking up a mixing bowl for the very first time, you'll be delighted how easy Junior's cheesecakes are to make—especially those in the Junior's Favorites chapter. We've collected facts, tips, and secrets from the professional bakers and our bake sessions to help you get started and keep you baking with success, every step of the way.

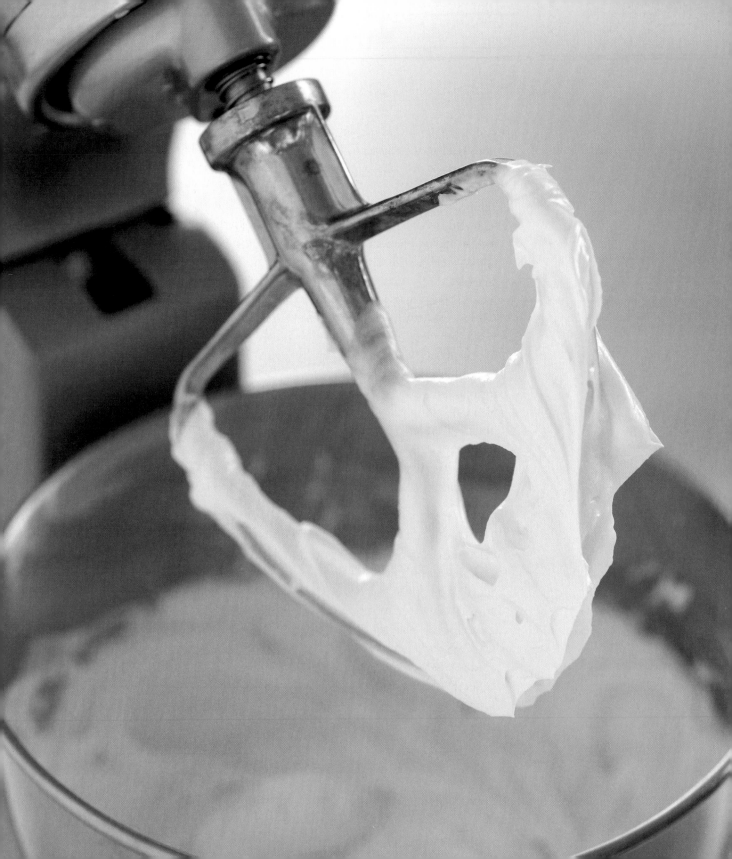

## Junior's Sponge Cake Crust

The Junior's cheesecake crust is a delicate sponge cake—the kind that you usually bake for birthday cakes. It's about ¼ inch thick, and has the slightest hint of vanilla and lemon. Use extra-large fresh eggs (or jumbo if you can find them). Let them warm up to room temperature so they whip up higher and give a lighter cake. The sugar adds tenderness and sweetness. Use cake flour, for a finer and more tender crumb, and sift it first with the baking powder and salt, then stir it in by hand, not with a mixer. All-purpose flour or self-rising flour just doesn't give the same light, delicious results. Don't forget the melted butter—it gives the cake a buttery flavor and that melt-in-your-mouth quality. It also ensures that your cake will be tender and creamy, not tough or crumbly.

For a light, tender sponge cake crust, whip the egg yolks first, by themselves without the whites, with an electric mixer on high speed for 3 minutes—time it! (Use the wire whisk attachment if your mixer has one.) Then gradually add half of the sugar and keep beating 5 minutes more, until thick, golden ribbons form in the bowl. Don't shortchange the beating time. Stir in the flour and blend in the butter by hand. Right before you pour the batter in the pan, fold in the egg whites, which you have beaten in another bowl with the rest of the sugar until they hold stiff peaks. Doing this forces lots of air bubbles into the batter, which expand during baking from the heat in the oven, causing the cake to rise and giving it a lighter and more delicate texture.

## Junior's Cheesecake Filling

The filling for Junior's cheesecake is not cakelike, but actually a smooth, satiny baked custard. This heavenly texture and flavor are the results of the ingredients—2 pounds of cream cheese, a couple of eggs, just the right amount of sugar for sweetness, a little cornstarch for stability, plenty of heavy whipping cream, and pure vanilla extract. Use only full-fat cream cheese, found in your grocer's dairy case in 8-ounce "bricks." Avoid using the soft or whipped varieties, lower-fat Neufchâtel, or fat-free cream cheese.

About 30 minutes before mixing the cake, let the cream cheese warm up to room temperature. Follow Junior's two-step mixing technique—it's one of their little-known secrets for making their cheesecake a cut above the rest.

**STEP ONE:** Cream together one 8-ounce package of the cream cheese with a little of the sugar and the cornstarch with the paddle attachment of an electric mixer on low speed to make a stable "starter-batter." Then add the rest of the cheese, one package at a time. Stop the mixer to scrape down the bowl after blending in each package and before adding the next.

**STEP TWO:** Increase the speed to medium, no faster! Beat in the remaining sugar, then the vanilla. Now blend in the eggs, one at a time, beating well after adding each one. Scrape down the bowl, then add the cream all at once. When the batter pulls together in the bowl and looks creamy, airy, almost billowy, it's ready to bake. Avoid overmixing!

### PREPARING THE PAN

For Junior's Original Cheesecake (page 36), use a 9-inch springform pan, preferably the nonstick kind. If it's a little larger than 9 inches, that's fine—but don't use a smaller pan unless you are making the 8-inch variation. A springform makes it much easier to remove the cheesecake without it cracking or falling apart. Check to make sure the spring clip on your pan still works and seals the rim tightly onto the bottom of the pan. (If it doesn't, replace the pan!) Butter the bottom and the sides well with softened butter, and be sure to use plenty of it.

And here's some advice from Alan Rosen: "When baking a cheesecake in a springform pan, first wrap the outside of the pan with heavy-duty aluminum foil. Be sure to wrap the bottom and all the way up the sides. This helps prevent water from seeping from the water bath into the cake pan during baking."

### PREHEATING THE OVEN

Use the conventional bake oven cycle—not convection. The hot circulating air in a convection oven can cause the cake to bake too fast, brown too much, and collapse in the center as it cools.

Junior's bakes its cheesecakes at 350°F. Preheat the oven at least half an hour before putting in the cake (some oven manufacturers recommend an hour so the temperature is steady and stable). Buy a good oven thermometer and keep it inside the oven to double-check the temperature before putting in the cake. Check your oven often. If the temperature fluctuates more than 25 degrees, call a repairman. An oven that holds its heat during the entire baking period is essential in baking a great cheesecake. If the temperature jumps too high, the cake can overbake, crack, and crumble; if it's too low, the cake might never firm up enough to slice it.

*The Junior's Way*

Here's a tip from Master Baker Michael Goodman: "Butter that's just softened, but not melted, adheres to the pan better. Also, if you lightly flour the buttered pan, the sides of the cake will unmold smoother."

### THE WATER BATH

Junior's always uses a water bath when baking cheesecakes. A water bath spreads out the heat evenly around the cake and adds moisture to the oven. The cake bakes gently, evenly, and slowly with moist heat. Your cheesecake will come out with golden-brown edges with a slightly golden-tan center—and no cracks. For the water bath, choose a pan that's larger than the springform and has sides at least as high. Place the cheesecake pan (wrapped with foil) in the center of the larger one. Add enough warm water to the water bath pan until it reaches halfway up the sides of the springform. Place the pans on the middle shelf of the oven.

Keep the door closed for the first 30 minutes of baking. "No one can resist peeking in the oven, but just look through the glass window," says Alan Rosen. "If you open the door before the cake has baked long enough to set, the rush of cold air can cause your cheesecake to fall." Check the water bath and add more warm water if necessary. If the water bath starts to boil, add a few ice cubes.

### NO CRACKS, PLEASE!

Junior's cheesecakes look professional *and* homemade—with smooth tops and no cracks. In addition to using a water bath, bake the cake at 350°F (no higher!), and watch so it doesn't overbake. If the cake bakes too long or at too high a temperature, the batter sets too fast and firms up too much, resulting in a dry crust on the top that cracks easily when you cut the cake. As the cake cools, the overbaked edges shrink and can cause a deep crack to form in the center.

### IS IT DONE YET?

Here's a tip from Junior's: take the cheesecake out of the oven when the edges are set and light golden brown and the top turns slightly golden tan and looks set and no longer wet. If it's still soft around the sides and the color is pale, leave the cake in the oven for five or ten minutes more.

### BRINGING THE CAKE OUT OF THE OVEN

First, carefully bring the water bath (with the cake still in it) out of the oven. Now, gently lift the cake out of the water bath and place it on a wire rack to cool (just leave the foil wrapped around it). If you leave the cake in the water bath, it will overbake. Be sure it's not in a draft. Alan Rosen says: "Just walk away, forget about it, and don't bother it for two hours!" It needs to rest, set, and cool. If it's moved or disturbed during this time, it could fall or crack.

*The Junior's Way*

The cornstarch in Junior's recipe helps ensure a perfectly baked cake, with no cracks. Cornstarch stabilizes the custard filling and helps prevent overcooking.

To remove your cheesecake
from the bottom of the
springform pan, place the
well-chilled cheesecake in
the freezer for 30 minutes,
no longer. If the cake has
already been frozen for
at least an hour, let it first
stand at room temperature
for 10 minutes before trying
to remove it from the pan.
Using a metal cake spatula
at least 12 inches long, lift
up the bottom edge of the
cake slightly, just enough
to release the vacuum holding the cake to the pan. If
the cake is still sticking, it
is because the butter used
to grease the pan has not
softened or melted. See tips
in "Chill Until Cold" on this
page.

## CHILL UNTIL COLD

After the cake has rested for a couple of hours, remove the foil but keep the
cake in the pan. (If the cake is still warm, refrigerate it unwrapped until it's no
longer warm to your touch.) Cover the cake with plastic wrap and refrigerate
until it's completely cold. This will take at least 4 hours, but if you have time,
chill it overnight.

To remove the cake from the pan easily, check to see if it has shrunken from the
sides of the pan. If not, run a small warm metal spatula or table knife around
the sides of the pan. Do this gently, moving the spatula up and down all around
the sides. Release the latch on the side of the pan. Now, holding the pan from
the bottom, push the cake up and away from the sides, letting the ring fall down
on your wrist. This keeps the sides of the cake looking smooth. To serve the
easiest way, keep the cake on the bottom of the pan and place on a serving plate.

If you want to remove the cake from the bottom of the pan, try this. Put the
cake (still in the pan) in the freezer for about half an hour—just long enough
to firm it up. Warm the bottom of the pan either by setting in on a hot wet towel
or on a low burner over very low heat for 10 to 15 seconds (just long enough
to melt the butter used to grease the pan but not long enough to make the pan
hot). Remove the sides of the pan (use potholders!). Now gently insert a long,
narrow metal spatula between the bottom of the cake and the pan, moving it
slowly in a circle. Then lift up the edge of the cake with the spatula, oh-so-gently,
just enough to release the vacuum between the bottom of the cake and the pan.
Using the spatula and your hands, gently lift the cake up slightly and slide it
onto the serving plate.

## Cheesecake Decorating Tips

First impressions mean a lot, especially when you're bringing out a homemade
cheesecake for your friends. With Junior's cheesecakes, good impressions are
guaranteed. When making the Original New York Cheesecake recipe, you need
only a nice cake plate to serve it on. But if you are serving one of the fancier
Junior's cakes and want to touch it up a bit, here are a few tips.

To straighten the sides of a cheesecake (after removing it from the pan), use
a flat metal icing spatula (about 1½ inches wide). Warm it under hot running
water, then smooth out the sides of the cold cake by gently running it around
the cake. Warm the spatula again a few times as you go. (If you're frosting

the sides with whipped cream, this same technique works.) If the cake rises unevenly in the oven, trim the top before decorating it. Chill the cake until it's cold and put it in the freezer about half an hour to firm it up. Using a long, sharp knife (a serrated one works fine here), carefully level the top of the cake with a back-and-forth sawing motion. Now brush away any crumbs on top.

Before drizzling the cake with melted chocolate or a whipped cream topping, remove the springform ring, leaving the cake on the bottom of the pan. Freeze the cake until it's firm and set (about half an hour if the cake is already cold). Place the cake on a serving plate and drizzle on the topping from the tip of a small pointed spoon (a grapefruit spoon with its pointed tip works well). Make the drizzles different lengths on the side of the cake. Since the cake is cold, the topping will freeze fast. (No unsightly pool of sauce on the plate!) Then refrigerate until serving time.

## For Professional Slices

For the cleanest, most professional cut, use a thin, sharp, straightedge slicing knife—not a serrated cake knife. Before making that first slice, warm the knife under hot running water and wipe it dry. After cutting each slice and before making the next one, wipe the knife clean with a warm wet towel. This technique makes every slice clean and picture perfect—just like it looks when they serve you a slice at Junior's.

If you and your friends and family can't eat all of the cake (hard to imagine!), freeze the rest. Wrap it in plastic wrap and freeze for up to six months. If you have decorated it with fresh fruits, remove them before wrapping the cake.

Take the cake out of the freezer the day before you plan to serve it and place it in the refrigerator (leave it all wrapped up). About two hours before serving, remove it from the refrigerator, unwrap it, place it on a serving plate, and return to the refrigerator to finish defrosting.

## Baking a Better Cheesecake

If your cheesecake doesn't come out quite as perfect as the picture, don't worry, it will still taste great! The common problems with baking any cake, especially a custardlike cheesecake, often result from a few simple things that are easy to avoid the next time you bake one. Here are a few common problems and how to solve them the next time around.

# If Your Cheesecake Is Not Perfect

| PROBLEM | PROBABLE CAUSES | SOLUTIONS |
|---|---|---|
| *1.* The top of my cheesecake cracked during baking. | • The ingredients were not mixed completely. The batter should be smooth—no lumps! | • Before putting the batter in the pan, stir it gently with a rubber spatula, lifting it up from the bottom and making sure all the ingredients are thoroughly mixed in and are wet. |
| | • The water bath was too hot.<br><br>• The water bath evaporated during baking, leaving the pan empty and the oven heat dry, instead of moist. Cheesecakes need moist heat during the complete baking cycle to bake evenly. | • Watch the water bath during baking and add a few ice cubes if the water boils.<br><br>• Do not let the water in the water bath bake dry.<br><br>• Add more warm water to the water bath if needed.<br><br>• Don't add cold water; the pan could warp. |
| | • The cake was overbaked. Your oven was probably too hot. | • Keep a good oven thermometer on your oven's middle shelf. Check the temperature often.<br><br>• Call your range repairman to recalibrate the oven. |
| *2.* I can't slide the cake off the bottom of the pan onto my cake plate. | • The cake needed to be slightly frozen (not just refrigerated) to firm up enough to remove it from the bottom of the pan. | • Refrigerate the cake until it's very cold. Then freeze for about 30 minutes.<br><br>First, remove the springform ring.<br><br>Next, warm the bottom of the pan on a low burner for 30 seconds, just long enough to melt the butter (which was used to grease the pan).<br><br>Now, slide a metal spatula between the bottom of the pan and the cake (releasing the vacuum), then lift and slide the cake onto the plate. |
| | | |

| PROBLEM | PROBABLE CAUSES | SOLUTIONS |
|---|---|---|
| *3.* My cheesecake fell a little in the center while it was cooling. | • Batter was beaten at too high a speed and/or for too long. | • When mixing the cheesecake filling, use only the low and medium speeds of the electric mixer.<br>• After adding the cream, mix the batter only until blended. Do not overmix. |
| | • The cake was underbaked and removed from the oven before it was done. | • Your cheesecake is done and ready to take out of the oven when the edges are golden brown and the top is an even, light golden tan. The top should look set and dry, not wet or sticky. |
| | • The cake was moved while it was still warm. | • Walk away and let the cake rest at room temperature for 2 hours before moving it. |
| | • You refrigerated the cake too soon.<br><br>• A cold draft of air hit the cake while it was cooling. | • Be sure the cake has cooled completely (at least 2 hours) before putting it into the refrigerator.<br>• Cool the cake away from open windows or doors and all air-conditioning vents. |
| *4.* The center of my cheesecake sank as it cooled. | • Cake was underbaked. | • Bake your next cake 5 to 10 minutes more. |
| | • Temperature inside your oven was too low. | • Keep a good oven thermometer on the middle shelf of your oven. Check the temperature often.<br>• Call your range repairman to recalibrate the oven. |
| *5.* The cake cut beautifully except it was a little soft in the center. | • The cake was slightly underbaked. | • "Don't worry—a cheesecake that's a little soft in the center is still delicious!" says Alan Rosen.<br>• Bake your next cake 5 to 10 minutes more. |
| | • Your oven was not holding the heat at the temperature you've set…it's too low. | • Keep a good oven thermometer on the middle shelf of your oven and check the temperature often.<br>• Call your range repairman to recalibrate the oven. |

| PROBLEM | PROBABLE CAUSES | SOLUTIONS |
|---|---|---|
| 6. My cheesecake cracked as it cooled. | • The batter was not mixed enough to dissolve the ingredients.<br>• Small lumps of cream cheese were left in the batter. | • Mix the batter until smooth and all the ingredients are thoroughly dissolved. |
| | • The cake baked too fast or too long, causing the cake to shrink as it cooled and leave a deep crack in the center. | • Check the cake after it has baked for an hour. If the edges are set and the center doesn't look wet, take it out. |
| | • The edges of the cake may have been stuck to the sides of the pan. | • If the cake has not shrunk from the sides of the pan after cooling the cake for 2 hours, gently run a warm small metal spatula around the sides. |
| | • The temperature inside your oven was probably too hot. | • Keep a good oven thermometer on your oven's middle shelf. Check the temperature often.<br>• Call your range repairman to recalibrate the oven. |
| 7. The sides of my cheesecake do not look as smooth or as pretty as they do in the photo. | • You may not have greased the sides of the pan well enough. | • Grease the sides of the pan generously with softened (not melted) butter, then lightly dust it with a little flour. |
| | • The cake stuck to the sides when it was being removed from the pan. | • Run a small metal spatula around the edge of the cake before releasing the springform clamp. |
| 8. The sponge cake crust is soggy. | • The cheesecake was still warm when you refrigerated it.<br>• Condensation (water droplets) became trapped in the cake, making it soggy. | • Let the cake cool at room temperature for at least 2 hours before refrigerating it.<br>• Do not wrap a warm cheesecake!<br>• If the cake feels even slightly warm, refrigerate it *unwrapped* for an hour or so before covering it with plastic wrap. |

*No one really knows just whose idea it was to use a sponge cake crust for Junior's cheesecake. It worked, and that same recipe continues to work today.*

# junior's sponge cake crust

**MAKES ONE 8- OR 9-INCH CRUST**

**FOR ONE 9-INCH CAKE CRUST:**

1/3 cup sifted cake flour

3/4 teaspoon baking powder

Pinch of salt

2 extra-large eggs, separated

1/3 cup sugar

1 teaspoon pure vanilla extract

2 drops pure lemon extract

2 tablespoons unsalted butter, melted

1/4 teaspoon cream of tartar

**FOR ONE 8-INCH CAKE CRUST:**

1/4 cup sifted cake flour

1/2 teaspoon baking powder

Pinch of salt

2 extra-large eggs, separated

1/4 cup sugar

3/4 teaspoon pure vanilla extract

2 drops pure lemon extract

2 tablespoons unsalted butter, melted

1/4 teaspoon cream of tartar

*1.* Preheat the oven to 350°F and generously butter the bottom and sides of a 8- or 9-inch springform pan (preferably a nonstick one). Wrap the outside with aluminum foil, covering the bottom and extending all the way up the sides.

*2.* In a small bowl, sift the flour, baking powder, and salt together.

*3.* Beat the egg yolks in a large bowl with an electric mixer on high for 3 minutes. With the mixer running, slowly add 2 tablespoons of the sugar and beat until thick light yellow ribbons form, about 5 minutes more. Beat in the extracts.

*4.* Sift the flour mixture over the batter and stir it in by hand, just until no more white flecks appear. Now, blend in the melted butter.

*5.* Now, wash the mixing bowl and beaters really well (if even a little fat is left, this can cause the egg whites not to whip). Put the egg whites and cream of tartar into the bowl and beat with the mixer on high until frothy. Gradually add the remaining sugar and continue beating until stiff peaks form (the whites will stand up and look glossy, not dry). Fold about one-third of the whites into the batter, then the remaining whites. Don't worry if you still see a few white specks, as they'll disappear during baking.

*6.* Gently spread out the batter over the bottom of the pan, and bake just until set and golden (not wet or sticky), about 10 minutes. Touch the cake gently in the center. If it springs back, it's done. Watch carefully and don't let the top brown. Leave the crust in the pan and place on a wire rack to cool. Leave the oven on while you prepare the batter.

### DARK CHOCOLATE SPONGE CAKE CRUST

Slice into some of Junior's cakes, especially the chocolaty ones, and you'll find a chocolate sponge cake on the bottom, instead of a golden sponge. The recipe and mixing techniques are the same, except you stir in 2 ounces of melted (see page 23) and slightly cooled bittersweet chocolate when you add the extracts.

*The Junior's Way*

Bake the cheesecake crust in the same springform pan you're using for the cheesecake. Watch the crust closely; since it's so thin, it needs only 10 to 12 minutes to bake.

*The Scottish were baking shortbread as far back as the twelfth century. It was baked in round pans that often had fluted edges, which looked like the fancy petticoats the ladies wore in court in those days; then it was cut into triangular wedges. Some still call these buttery, delicious shortbread cookies "petticoat tails" today. Junior's has turned this popular cookie into a rich crust for a few of their fanciest cheesecakes.*

# junior's shortbread crust

**MAKES ONE 9-INCH CRUST**

1 cup all-purpose flour

1 tablespoon cornstarch

¼ teaspoon salt

½ cup (1 stick) unsalted butter, at room temperature

⅓ cup sugar

2 extra-large egg yolks

2 teaspoons pure vanilla extract

*1.* Preheat the oven to 350°F and generously butter the bottom and sides of a 9-inch springform pan. Wrap the outside with aluminum foil, covering the bottom and extending all the way up the sides. Mix the flour, cornstarch, and salt together.

*2.* In a medium-size bowl, beat the butter and sugar together with an electric mixer on high until creamy. Add the egg yolks and vanilla and beat until blended. Reduce the speed to low and mix in the flour mixture just until it disappears and a dough forms. Work the dough with your hands until it comes together in a ball. Chill about 30 minutes if you have the time.

*3.* Flour your hands, then place the dough in the center of the pan and begin pressing with the heels of your hands from the center outward toward the edges, working in a circular motion around the pan and up the sides. Keep pressing until the crust is flat on the bottom and stands up about 1½ inches on the sides. Pinch the edge between your two index fingers to give a fluted effect. Prick the crust in several places with a dinner fork (this lets the crust bake more evenly without rising up from the pan).

*4.* Bake the crust just until it's set and golden (do not overbake!), about 15 minutes. Leave the crust in the pan and place on a wire rack to cool. Leave the oven on while you prepare the batter.

## The Junior's Way

If you have time, chill the dough about half an hour before pressing it into the pan. This makes it easier to work with.

*Here's another Junior's buttery, melt-in-your-mouth shortbread, but this time you'll have enough dough to make a large tart crust.*

# all-butter tart crust

**MAKES ONE 11- OR 12-INCH TART CRUST**

1⅓ cups all-purpose flour
½ teaspoon salt
¾ cup (1½ sticks) unsalted butter, at room temperature
½ cup sugar
1 extra-large egg yolk
1 teaspoon pure vanilla extract

*1.* Preheat the oven to 350°F. Generously butter the bottom and sides of an 11- or 12-inch tart pan (preferably a nonstick one) with a removable bottom and fluted sides at least 1 inch high. Wrap the outside with aluminum foil, covering the bottom and all the way up the sides of the pan.

*2.* In a medium-size bowl, mix the flour and salt together.

*3.* In a large bowl, beat the butter and sugar together with an electric mixer on high until creamy. Add the egg yolk and vanilla and beat until blended. Reduce the speed to low and mix in the flour just until it disappears and a dough forms. Work the dough with your hands until it comes together in a ball. Chill about 30 minutes if you have the time.

*4.* Flour your hands and put the dough in the center of the pan. Using the heels of your hands, press the dough into the bottom of the pan and up the sides. Work in a circular motion from the center out to the edge and try to achieve an even thickness. Prick the crust in several places with a dinner fork (the crust will bake more evenly).

*5.* Bake just until the crust sets and turns golden (do not overbake!), about 10 minutes. Leave the crust in the pan and transfer the pan to a wire rack to cool. Leave the oven on while you prepare the batter.

## The Junior's Way

Don't worry about handling this dough too much. It's so rich that you're guaranteed a buttery and flaky crust every time. Right before baking, take out a rolling pin and roll it gently across the top edge of the tart pan. Any excess pastry dough will fall away. This gives the baked shell sharp, clean edges and a professional finish.

*Not a brownie, not a shortbread either—but something deliciously in-between. This crust bakes into a decadent chocolate cookie that goes great with a cheesecake filling and slices perfectly. Try substituting this for the sponge cake crust in the Triple Chocolate Cheesecake, on page 106.*

# brownie shortbread cookie crust

**MAKES ONE 9-INCH CRUST**

1 cup plus 2 tablespoons
all-purpose flour

1/4 teaspoon salt

1/2 cup (1 stick) unsalted butter,
at room temperature

1/3 cup sugar

1 extra-large egg yolk

1 teaspoon pure vanilla extract

2 tablespoons bittersweet
or semisweet chocolate, melted
(see page 23)

*1.* Preheat the oven to 350°F and generously butter the bottom and sides of a 9-inch springform pan. Wrap the outside with aluminum foil, covering the bottom and extending all the way up the sides. Mix the flour and salt together.

*2.* In a medium-size bowl, beat the butter and sugar together with an electric mixer on high until creamy. Blend in the egg yolk and vanilla, then the melted chocolate. Reduce the speed to low and mix in the flour just until it disappears and a dough forms.

*3.* Push the dough over the bottom of the pan with a rubber spatula. Flour your hands, then smooth out the dough evenly to the edge of the pan with your fingertips, working in a circular motion. Do not press up the sides.

*4.* Bake the crust just until it's set and forms a light brown crust on top (do not overbake!), about 15 minutes. Leave the crust in the pan and place on a wire rack to cool.

## The Junior's Way

This is a sticky dough, so flour your hands well and pat the dough out evenly to the edge. Do not push it up the sides.

*At Junior's, the bakers often use dark chocolate curls to decorate cheesecakes for a delicious and very professional looking finish.*

# chocolate curls

**MAKES ENOUGH TO GENEROUSLY DECORATE ONE 9-INCH CHEESECAKE**

8 ounces bittersweet
or semisweet chocolate or
white chocolate

**FOR LARGE CHOCOLATE CURLS:**

Melt the chocolate over low heat. Spread it out in a thin sheet on a flat surface—but not so thin that you can see the surface through the chocolate. If you have a marble slab, use it. If not, use a baking sheet. Let the chocolate cool. Using a baker's bench scraper or a wide, flat metal spatula, scrape up the chocolate into wide curls, lifting them up as you work. The curls will be different widths and lengths, but that's fine. If the chocolate curls up into one long sheet, let it cool more before scraping again. Carefully place the curls where you want them on the cake. If you are decorating the side of the cake with them, press the curls gently into the frosting with your fingers so they stay, without falling off.

**FOR SMALLER CHOCOLATE CURLS:**

Buy a thick bar of chocolate and use at room temperature (not straight from the refrigerator). Stand up the chocolate bar vertically, slightly on an angle, against a flat surface, such as a chopping board. Slowly scrape down the bar with a vegetable peeler, allowing the chocolate to fall away into a pile of soft curls. Using a wide, flat metal spatula, carefully place them on the cake.

### The Junior's Way

When making dark chocolate curls, use dark semisweet or bittersweet rather than milk chocolate. They give more of a color contrast and stand out better on the cake.

*Here is a decorating secret shared by Master Baker Michael Goodman: "When I want a fast finishing for a cheesecake, there's nothing better than a traditional chocolate ganache. All you need is a good dark chocolate, some heavy cream, and a splash of good vanilla. It's ready in minutes."*

# traditional chocolate ganache

**MAKES ENOUGH TO DECORATE ONE 9-INCH CHEESECAKE (TOP AND SIDES)**

8 ounces bittersweet chocolate, coarsely chopped

1 cup cold heavy or whipping cream

1 teaspoon pure vanilla extract

*1.* Combine the chocolate and cream in a medium-size saucepan and stir over medium-low heat until the chocolate melts and the mixture begins to bubble a little around the sides. Quickly whisk the mixture until it comes together in a smooth chocolate sauce.

*2.* Remove from the heat and whisk in the vanilla. Pour into a heatproof bowl that can go into the freezer. Chill the ganache in the freezer just until it thickens, about 15 minutes. Use immediately to glaze the top of a cheesecake. Let some ganache drizzle down the sides—or, if you wish, frost the sides completely, using a narrow metal icing spatula. Do not cover. Return the cake to the freezer for 1 hour before cutting.

## The Junior's Way

First freeze the cheesecake at least an hour so it's icy cold; that way the ganache will set up fast on the cake. Then spoon the chilled ganache on top of the cake, pushing it just to the edge.

*A traditional ganache is a smooth, pourable mixture made from heavy cream and bittersweet chocolate. It's often used in bakeries to give a velvety coating on a cake. Junior's also makes this whipped cream version.*

# whipped chocolate ganache

**ENOUGH TO DECORATE ONE 9-INCH CHEESECAKE (TOP AND SIDES)**

⅓ cup sugar

3 tablespoons unsweetened cocoa powder

1 cup cold heavy or whipping cream

1 teaspoon pure vanilla extract

*1.* In a small bowl, toss the sugar with the cocoa and set aside. In a medium-size bowl, whip the cream with an electric mixer on high until the cream thickens and soft peaks just begin to form. While the mixer is still running, add the sugar-cocoa mixture, then the vanilla.

*2.* Continue beating just until the cream turns a light-chocolate color and stiff peaks form. Watch carefully and do not overbeat at this stage (the cream might curdle). Use immediately for frosting a cake or piping decorations or cover with plastic wrap and store in the refrigerator until ready to serve. Best when used within 1 day.

### FOR CHOCOLATE ROSETTES:

To make chocolate rosettes, fit the bag with a medium or large star tip (a closed-star tip gives fancier rosettes). Put the cake in the freezer just for 30 minutes to set the decorations. Transfer to the refrigerator until ready to serve.

*The Junior's Way*

Use a medium star tip for piping shells, stars, and fleur-de-lis rosettes of whipped chocolate ganache on top of the cake. Choose an open-star tip #32 or closed-star tip #35 for fancier decorations and a large star tip (#199) for making rosettes around the top or bottom edge of the cake.

*Junior's uses a lot of whipped cream. Take a tip from the bakers: stabilize the whipped cream to make this decorator's version. It's much easier to work with and holds its shape perfectly. We found that beating in a little melted gelatin works well. At Junior's, they a use a certified kosher stablizer (not gelatin). If this is a concern for you, ask your local kosher grocer for a gelatin replacement.*

# decorator's whipped cream

**MAKES ENOUGH TO DECORATE THE TOP OF ONE 9-INCH CHEESECAKE**
**(DOUBLE THE RECIPE TO FROST AND DECORATE THE TOP AND SIDES OF ONE 9-INCH CAKE)**

1 teaspoon unflavored granulated gelatin
1 tablespoon cold water
1 cup cold heavy or whipping cream
1 tablespoon sugar
1 teaspoon pure vanilla extract

*1.* Place the gelatin in a heatproof measuring cup, stir in the cold water, and let stand until it swells and thickens (this takes only about 1 minute). Cook the gelatin in the microwave on high for about 30 seconds or over a pan of simmering water for about 1 minute, until clear and completely melted.

*2.* In a medium-size bowl, whip the cream with an electric mixer on high until it thickens and soft peaks just begin to form. With the mixer still running, add the sugar and beat just until the cream stands up in peaks (don't overmix or the cream will curdle). Beat in the vanilla. Now, add the melted gelatin all at once and beat until thoroughly incorporated. Refrigerate for at least 30 minutes but not more than 1 hour. Use immediately as a cake filling or frosting or refrigerate.

**FOR WHIPPED CREAM ROSETTES:**
Fit a pastry bag with a large closed-star tip (#133) or a large open-star tip (#199). Half-fill the bag with the whipped cream and pipe large rosettes all around the top or bottom edge of the cake. For smaller decorative stars and rosettes, use a medium closed-star tip (such as #27, #31 or #35) or a medium open-star tip (such as #22 or #32). The closed-star tips create deeper grooves and more details than the open-star ones, but both work fine. Put the cake in the freezer for 30 minutes to set the decorations. Transfer to the refrigerator until time to serve.

### The Junior's Way

Fill the pastry bag only half full with whipped cream, then twist it tightly near the top. Squeeze a little cream back into the bowl until the pocket of air near the tip escapes. Lightly squeeze the bag. You're now ready to decorate any way you wish.

A slice of Brownie Swirl cheesecake (page 108), topped with a whipped cream rosette.

*This recipe takes basic buttercream frosting to a new level. It begins with confectioners' sugar and butter, but the extra butter and a little light corn syrup create a light, creamy, airy, almost fluffy consistency that's great for piping and swirling onto a cake. If you do a lot of cake decorating, buy a set of icing colors, which resemble thick coloring pastes. Liquid food colors work too, but they are available in fewer colors. Use a toothpick or the pointed tip of a knife to add color to icing—you need only a small amount!*

# decorator's buttercream

**MAKES ENOUGH TO DECORATE ONE 9-INCH CHEESECAKE (TOP AND SIDES)**

4 cups sifted confectioners' sugar (about 1 pound)

¼ teaspoon salt

1 cup (2 sticks) unsalted butter, at room temperature

1 tablespoon light corn syrup

1 tablespoon pure vanilla extract

¼ to ⅓ cup heavy or whipping cream

Assorted food colors (optional)

*1.* Sift the confectioners' sugar and salt together in a large bowl.

*2.* In another large bowl, cream the butter with an electric mixer on high until light yellow and slightly thickened, about 3 minutes. With the mixer still running, beat in the corn syrup and vanilla. Reduce the mixer to low and beat in the sugar in two additions, beating well after each. Blend in ¼ cup of the cream all at once until the frosting is spreading consistency, adding a little more cream if needed.

*3.* Return the mixer speed to high and whip until light and creamy, about 3 minutes more. If you want different colors of frosting, divide into three or four small bowls. To tint the frosting, add a small amount of color at first and blend it in completely before adding more.

*4.* Fit a pastry bag with a small round tip (#2 or #3) for lines; a small open-star tip (#16 or #17) for small stars; a medium closed-star tip (#27, #31 or #35) or a medium open-star tip (#22 or #32) for stars, shell borders, fleur-de-lis, rosettes, or zigzag lines; or a large open-star tip (#199) for finishing off the top or bottom edge of a large cake with rosettes.

## The Junior's Way

**Work fast! If the icing gets a little too soft during piping, place the bag in the refrigerator for just a few minutes. Watch it carefully and remove before it firms up too much.**

*Junior's uses this topping on many of its fruit cheesecakes. It's buttery, crumbly, and tastes just like the crumb topping my grandmother used for her apple pies.*

# junior's cinnamon crumb topping

**MAKES ENOUGH TO TOP ONE 9-INCH CHEESECAKE**

¾ cup all-purpose flour

⅓ cup firmly packed light brown sugar

½ teaspoon ground cinnamon

Grated rind of 1 large lemon (about 1 teaspoon)

½ cup (1 stick) cold unsalted butter, cut into small pieces

*1.* Preheat the oven to 350°F. Generously butter a jellyroll pan or a 9 x 13-inch baking pan.

*2.* Mix the flour, brown sugar, cinnamon, and lemon rind together in a medium-size bowl. Work in the butter with your fingers until coarse crumbs form.

*3.* Spread out the crumbs in the pan. Bake until the topping is golden brown, bubbly, and slightly crunchy, about 15 minutes, tossing the mixture with a spatula 2 or 3 times. Watch it carefully. It's ready when it turns a light golden brown (do not let it brown too much). Let the mixture cool in the pan on a wire rack for at least 30 minutes, then break into fine crumbs. (If you have any extra topping, put in a zip-top plastic bag and freeze for up to 1 month. It's great over ice cream!)

## The Junior's Way

**Cut the stick of butter into 16 pieces by first cutting the stick across horizontally into 2 rectangles, then each into 8 smaller equal pieces.**

*Here's an easy way to decorate a Junior's cheesecake. Pick a perfect strawberry and turn it into a flower in seconds. Use just one for the center or scatter three on the top, close to the edge of the cake.*

# strawberry flower

**EACH LARGE STRAWBERRY MAKES ONE FLOWER**

*1.* Wash the berry right before you're ready to make the flower and dry it well on a paper towel. Place the berry horizontally, on its side, on a cutting board. Choose a sharp fruit or paring knife with a thin straight-edged blade. Starting at the pointed end of the berry and cutting toward, but not through, the green cap, make 2 or 3 horizontal cuts, dividing the berry into 3 or 4 "petals." Stop cutting before reaching the green cap, keeping the berry in one piece. If you cut all the way through the berry, the petals will fall off.

*2.* Gently fan out the petals slightly into a decorative strawberry flower. Arrange a few strawberry flowers on top of a whole cake or place one berry beside each slice of cake on an individual dessert plate.

*The bakers at Junior's never waste anything in their bakery—especially strawberries! They carefully choose the most perfect berries for decorating their strawberry cheesecakes. The rest ends up in this delicious sauce that they spoon over every slice of strawberry shortcake, over their mile-high strawberry sundaes, and, on special request, over a slice of their plain cheesecake.*

# junior's signature strawberry sauce

**MAKES 1 QUART**

2 quarts fresh ripe strawberries
1 cup cold water
1 cup sugar
2 tablespoons cornstarch
1 teaspoon pure vanilla extract
¼ teaspoon pure lemon extract
2 to 3 drops red food coloring (optional)

*1.* Wash, hull, and dry the strawberries on paper towels. Slice them ½ inch thick, vertically from top to tip, into a large bowl.

*2.* Bring ¾ cup of the water and all the sugar to a boil in a medium-size saucepan over high heat and let boil for 5 minutes.

*3.* Dissolve the cornstarch in the remaining ¼ cup water in a cup. Whisk this mixture into the boiling syrup and cook until the mixture thickens and turns clear, about 2 minutes. Remove from the heat, stir in the extracts and food coloring, if you like.

*4.* Drizzle over the berries and toss lightly to coat. Store, tightly covered, in the refrigerator up to 3 days or in the freezer for up to 1 month.

# Junior's Favorites

If you've never had a slice of Junior's cheesecake (and even if you have and already know how fabulous it tastes!), turn to the first recipe and bake up an Original New York Cheesecake. As the name implies, the recipe hasn't changed since 1950 — it's the same creamy cake on a delicate sponge cake crust that made Junior's famous. Naturally, it's still the number-one favorite among Junior's regular customers. But that same cheesecake mounded with fresh strawberries, glistening with strawberry glaze, and laden with macaroon crunch is a close second. The bakers at Junior's are also known for swirling all kinds of delicious extras into their original cheesecake filling to create even more fabulous taste sensations — from bittersweet chocolate to strawberries, raspberries, peanut butter, even pumpkin. You'll find them all here — and the list keeps growing!

*Surprisingly, this is one of the easiest cakes to make. Follow this recipe from Junior's that we have specially adapted for your home kitchen and you'll soon be slicing up the best cheesecake you've ever tasted. Alan Rosen explains what makes it so special: "It's light but not crumbly, oh-so-creamy but not dense, and with that heavenly cream cheese flavor that makes Junior's New York cheesecake famous the world over."*

# original new york cheesecake

**MAKES ONE 9-INCH CHEESECAKE, ABOUT 2 1/2 INCHES HIGH**

1 recipe 9-inch Junior's
Sponge Cake Crust (page 17)

Four 8-ounce packages
cream cheese (use only full fat),
at room temperature

1 2/3 cups sugar

1/4 cup cornstarch

1 tablespoon pure vanilla extract

2 extra-large eggs

3/4 cup heavy or whipping cream

*1.* Preheat the oven to 350°F. Generously butter the bottom and sides of a 9-inch springform pan. Wrap the outside with aluminum foil, covering the bottom and extending all the way up the sides. Make and bake the cake crust and leave it in the pan. Keep the oven on.

*2.* Put one package of the cream cheese, 1/3 cup of the sugar, and the cornstarch in a large bowl and beat with an electric mixer on low until creamy, about 3 minutes, scraping down the bowl several times. Blend in the remaining cream cheese, one package at a time, scraping down the bowl after each one.

*3.* Increase the mixer speed to medium and beat in the remaining 1 1/3 cups sugar, then the vanilla. Blend in the eggs, one at a time, beating well after adding each one. Beat in the cream just until completely blended. Be careful not to overmix! Gently spoon the batter over the crust.

*4.* Place the cake in a large shallow pan containing hot water that comes about 1 inch up the sides of the springform. Bake until the edges are light golden brown and the top is slightly golden tan, about 1 1/4 hours. Remove the cheesecake from the water bath, transfer to a wire rack, and let cool for 2 hours (just walk away—don't move it). Then, leave the cake in the pan, cover loosely with plastic wrap, and refrigerate until completely cold, preferably overnight or for at least 4 hours.

*5.* To serve, release and remove the sides of the springform, leaving the cake on the bottom of the pan. Place on a cake plate. Refrigerate until ready to serve. Slice the cold cake with a sharp straight-edge knife, not a serrated one. Cover any leftover cake and refrigerate or wrap and freeze for up to 1 month.

**TO MAKE AN 8-INCH CAKE:**

Make an 8-inch sponge cake crust and use the cheesecake filling ingredient amounts as follows: three 8-ounce packages cream cheese, 1⅓ cups sugar, 3 tablespoons cornstarch, 1 tablespoon pure vanilla extract, 2 extra-large eggs, and ⅔ cup heavy or whipping cream. The cooking time will be about the same.

*The Junior's Way*

Master Baker Michael Goodman says: "Always bake the cheesecake in a water bath, as we do here at Junior's. It keeps the heat in the oven moist and helps the cake bake slowly, gently, and evenly. This helps ensure that your cheese-cake comes out of the oven with a smooth top— and no large cracks."

*This is another favorite at Junior's. It comes to your table with ruby red circles of strawberry purée swirled throughout. I like to decorate the top with fresh strawberry slices, slightly slanting and overlapping, around the edge of the cake. First brush the top outside edge of the cake with a little cream, and then arrange the berries. The cream helps hold the berries in place.*

# strawberry swirl cheesecake

**MAKES ONE 9-INCH CHEESECAKE, ABOUT 2½ INCHES HIGH**

1 recipe 9-inch Junior's
Sponge Cake Crust (page 17)

10 ounces (about 1 cup)
dry-pack frozen whole strawberries
(unsweetened, not in syrup),
thawed and drained well

5 tablespoons cornstarch

Three 8-ounce packages
cream cheese (use only full fat),
at room temperature

1⅓ cups sugar

1 tablespoon pure vanilla extract

2 extra-large eggs

⅔ cup heavy or whipping cream,
plus 1 tablespoon for brushing

1 quart large ripe fresh strawberries

*1.* Preheat the oven to 350°F. Generously butter the bottom and sides of a 9-inch springform pan. Wrap the outside with aluminum foil, covering the bottom and extending all the way up the sides.   Make and bake the cake crust and leave it in the pan. Keep the oven on.

*2.* Pulse the thawed strawberries in your food processor until smooth (you need ¾ cup of strawberry purée).  Stir in 1 tablespoon of the cornstarch and set aside. It will thicken slightly as it stands.

*3.* Put one package of the cream cheese, ⅓ cup of the sugar, and the remaining 4 tablespoons cornstarch in a large bowl. Beat with an electric mixer on low until creamy, about 3 minutes, scraping the bowl down several times. Blend in the remaining cream cheese, one package at a time, scraping down the bowl after each one. Increase the mixer speed to medium and beat in the remaining 1 cup sugar, then the vanilla. Blend in the eggs, one at a time, beating well after adding each one. Beat in ⅔ cup of the cream just until completely blended. Be careful not to overmix! Gently spoon the batter on top of the crust.

*4.* Using a teaspoon, drop the strawberry purée in small spoonfuls on top of the batter, pushing it down slightly as you go. Using a thin, pointed knife, cut through the batter a few times in a "figure 8" design, just until red swirls appear (don't mix in the purée completely or the whole cake will turn pink and you'll lose the swirls).

*5.* Place the cake in a large shallow pan containing hot water that comes about 1 inch up the sides of the springform. Bake until the edges are light golden brown and the top is slightly golden tan with strawberry swirls, about 1¼ hours. Remove the cheesecake from the water bath, transfer to a wire rack, and let cool for 2 hours (just walk away—don't move it). Leave the cake in the pan, cover loosely with plastic wrap, and refrigerate until completely cold, preferably overnight or at least 4 hours.

*6.* While the cake chills, wash and hull the fresh strawberries and slice them ¼ inch thick from top to tip (not crosswise), reserving the biggest, prettiest berry for the center.

*7.* To serve, release and remove the sides of the springform, leaving the cake on the bottom of the pan. Place on a cake plate. Brush the top outer rim of the cake with the remaining 1 tablespoon cream (this helps the berries stay where you put them instead of falling off the edge). Arrange the sliced strawberries in a ring on top, with tips pointing outward, angling and overlapping the berries as you go. Refrigerate until ready to serve. Slice the cold cake with a sharp straight-edge knife, not a serrated one. Cover any leftover cake and refrigerate it, or remove the fresh berry decorations, then wrap and freeze for up to 1 month.

*No matter when I go to the bakery, chances are good these cheesecakes are either coming out of the oven or being decorated or packed for shipping. And for good reason—this is one of their most popular cakes. It's Junior's famous creamy New York cheesecake crowned with plenty of juicy fresh berries, glistening with a shiny strawberry glaze, and finished with crunchy macaroon crumbs decorating the edge. Over-the-top delicious!*

# *fresh strawberry cheesecake with macaroon crunch*

**MAKES ONE 9-INCH CHEESECAKE, ABOUT 3 INCHES HIGH**

1 recipe 9-inch Junior's
Sponge Cake Crust (page 17)

Three 8-ounce packages
cream cheese (use only full fat),
at room temperature

1 1/3 cups sugar

3 tablespoons cornstarch

1 tablespoon pure vanilla extract

2 extra-large eggs

2/3 cup heavy or whipping cream

**FOR THE MACAROON CRUNCH:**

1/2 cup chopped blanched almonds

1/2 cup chopped walnuts

1/3 cup sweetened
shredded coconut

*(continued on page 41)*

*1.* Preheat the oven to 350°F. Generously butter the bottom and sides of a 9-inch springform pan. Wrap the outside with aluminum foil, covering the bottom and extending all the way up the sides. Make and bake the cake crust and leave it in the pan. Keep the oven on.

*2.* Put one package of the cream cheese, 1/3 cup of the sugar, and the cornstarch in a large bowl and beat with an electric mixer on low until creamy, about 3 minutes, scraping down the bowl several times. Blend in the remaining cream cheese, one package at a time, scraping down the bowl after each one. Increase the mixer speed to medium and beat in the remaining 1 cup sugar, then the vanilla. Blend in the eggs, one at a time, beating well after adding each one. Beat in the cream just until completely blended. Be careful not to overmix! Gently spoon the batter over the crust.

*3.* Place the cake in a large shallow pan containing hot water that comes about 1 inch up the sides of the springform. Bake until the edges are light golden brown and the top is slightly golden tan, about 1¼ hours. Remove the cheese-

cake from the water bath, transfer to a wire rack, and let the cake cool for 2 hours (just walk away—don't move it). Leave the cake in the pan, cover loosely with plastic wrap, and refrigerate until completely cold, preferably overnight or at least 4 hours.

*4.* Meanwhile, make the macaroon crunch. Check that the oven is preheated to 350°F and that the water bath has been removed. Toss the nuts and coconut together and spread out on a jellyroll pan or baking sheet. Toast until crunchy and golden, 10 to 15 minutes, tossing a couple of times. Set aside to cool.

*5.* Make the strawberry topping. Wash and hull the strawberries, then dry with paper towels. Process 1 cup of the least attractive berries in a food processor until smooth (you need ½ cup of purée). Decorate the completely chilled cake (still in the pan) with the remaining whole berries. Starting at the outside edge, arrange them with their tips pointing up, or on their sides, with their tips pointing to the edge, as they do at Junior's. Continue until the top of the cake is completely covered with berries. And for an extra touch, add an extra cluster of berries in the center, if you wish.

*6.* Stir the strawberry jelly, apricot preserves, and corn syrup together in a small saucepan over medium-low heat until melted. Blend in the ½ cup strawberry purée. In a small cup, completely dissolve the cornstarch in the cold water, then whisk into the glaze mixture. Bring to a simmer and cook until the mixture boils, thickens, and turns clear, about 2 minutes. Strain the glaze and drizzle over the berries, covering them completely, letting a little drizzle over the sides. Loosely cover the cake (still in the pan) with plastic wrap, making sure the glaze does not stick to the wrap. Refrigerate until completely cold and the glaze has set, at least 2 hours.

*7.* To serve, release and remove the sides of the springform, leaving the cake on the bottom of the pan. Sprinkle a little of the macaroon crunch over all of the berries. If you like, you can also add another finishing touch of a solid border of crunch around the outside edge of the cake. Return to the refrigerator until serving time. Slice the cold cake with a sharp straight-edge knife, not a serrated one. Cover any leftover cake and refrigerate it. Do not freeze this cake.

*The Junior's Way*

Pick through the strawberries and choose the most attractive ones which are similar in size. Save these for decorating the top and purée the remaining ones to make the strawberry topping.

FOR THE STRAWBERRY TOPPING:
2 quarts large ripe strawberries
1 cup strawberry jelly
½ cup apricot preserves
1 tablespoon light corn syrup
1 tablespoon cornstarch
1 tablespoon cold water

*Here's the original Junior's cheesecake, made even better with the addition of vanilla beans. Since it can be difficult to grind vanilla beans at home, I like to make vanilla sugar instead by burying the bean pod overnight in the granulated sugar I intend to use. The sugar turns fragrant with a strong vanilla taste. Save the bean for decorating the cake, then use later in some other recipe if you wish.*

# vanilla bean cheesecake

**MAKES ONE 9-INCH CHEESECAKE, ABOUT 2½ INCHES HIGH**

1²/₃ cups granulated sugar

1 vanilla bean (about 7 inches long)

1 recipe 9-inch Junior's
Sponge Cake Crust (page 17)

Four 8-ounce packages
cream cheese (use only full fat),
at room temperature

¼ cup cornstarch

1 tablespoon pure vanilla extract

2 extra-large eggs

¾ cup heavy or whipping cream

One half-pint fresh raspberries
(about 6 ounces)

Confectioners' sugar

*1.* The night before you plan to make this cake, put the granulated sugar in a small bowl and bury the vanilla bean in it, covering it completely. Cover tightly with plastic wrap and let stand overnight to flavor the sugar. When you're ready to make the cake, set the vanilla bean aside to decorate the center of the cake.

*2.* Preheat the oven to 350°F. Generously butter the bottom and sides of a 9-inch springform pan. Wrap the outside with aluminum foil, covering the bottom and extending all the way up the sides. Make and bake the cake crust and leave it in the pan. Keep the oven on.

*3.* Put one package of the cream cheese, ⅓ cup of the vanilla-flavored sugar, and the cornstarch in a large bowl. Beat with an electric mixer on low until creamy, about 3 minutes, scraping the bowl down several times. Blend in the remaining cream cheese, one package at a time, scraping down the bowl after each one. Increase the mixer speed to medium and beat in the remaining 1⅓ cups vanilla sugar, then the vanilla. Blend in the eggs, one at a time, beating well after adding each one. Beat in the cream just until completely blended. Be careful not to overmix! Gently spoon the batter on top of the crust.

*4.* Place the cake in a large shallow pan containing hot water that comes about 1 inch up the sides of the springform. Bake until the edges are light golden brown and the top is slightly golden tan, about 1¼ hours. Remove the cheesecake from the water bath, transfer to a wire rack, and let the cake cool for

2 hours (just walk away—don't move it). Leave the cake in the pan, cover loosely with plastic wrap, and refrigerate until completely cold, preferably overnight or at least 4 hours.

*5.* Wash and drain the raspberries and place them on paper towels to dry (very important!). Release and remove the sides of the springform, leaving the cake on the bottom of the pan. Place on a cake plate. Put some confectioners' sugar in a tea strainer and sift enough over the top of the cake to evenly cover it with a fine dusting. (Don't worry if some falls onto edge of the cake plate— it looks great!) Decorate the top with a circle of the raspberries about 2 inches from the rim, pointing the tips up. Stand up a small cluster of berries in the center. For a nice finishing touch, dust the vanilla bean with a little extra sugar, tie it in a loose knot, and stand it up against the berries in the center of the cake. Refrigerate until ready to serve. Slice the cold cake with a sharp straight-edge knife, not a serrated one. Cover any leftover cake and refrigerate, or remove the decorations, wrap, and freeze for up to 1 month.

## The Junior's Way

For the best flavor possible, use only the freshest vanilla bean for making the vanilla sugar. Fresh vanilla beans feel slightly oily and have a rich aroma. Older beans are shriveled, dry, and brittle, with little flavor to transfer to the sugar.

# cappuccino cheesecake

1 recipe 9-inch Junior's
Sponge Cake Crust (page 17)

1 tablespoon instant freeze-dried
espresso or coffee

1 tablespoon hot water

Four 8-ounce packages
cream cheese (use only full fat),
at room temperature

1 2/3 cups sugar

1/3 cup cornstarch

1 tablespoon pure vanilla extract

2 extra-large eggs

3/4 cup heavy or whipping cream

Chocolate Curls (page 21)

1 tablespoon unsweetened
cocoa powder

Coffee beans (optional)

MAKES ONE 9-INCH CHEESECAKE, ABOUT 2 1/2 INCHES HIGH

*1.* Preheat the oven to 350°F. Generously butter the bottom and sides of a 9-inch springform pan. Wrap the outside with aluminum foil, covering the bottom and extending all the way up the sides. Make and bake the cake crust and leave it in the pan. Keep the oven on.

*2.* Dissolve the instant espresso in the hot water in a small cup and let stand. Put one package of the cream cheese, 1/3 cup of the sugar, and the cornstarch in a large bowl. Beat with an electric mixer on low until creamy, about 3 minutes, scraping the bowl down several times. Blend in the remaining cream cheese, one package at a time, scraping down the bowl after each one. Increase the mixer speed to medium and beat in the remaining 1 1/3 cups sugar, then the vanilla. Blend in the eggs, one at a time, beating well after adding each one. Stir the dissolved coffee into the cream, then beat into the cream cheese mixture just until completely blended. Be careful not to overmix! Gently spoon the batter on top of the cake crust.

*3.* Place the cake in a large shallow pan containing hot water that comes about 1 inch up the sides of the springform. Bake until the edges are light golden brown and the top is light tan, about 1 1/4 hours. Remove the cheesecake from the water bath, transfer to a wire rack, and let the cake cool for 2 hours (just walk away—don't move it). Leave the cake in the pan, cover loosely with plastic wrap, and refrigerate until completely cold, preferably overnight or at least 4 hours.

*4.* To decorate, release and remove the sides of the springform, leaving the cake on the bottom of the pan. Place on a cake plate (choose one that can go into the freezer). Put the jelly and corn syrup in a small saucepan and stir constantly over low heat just until pourable (don't let it boil). Take the cake out of the freezer and spoon the jelly over the top (don't worry if a little drips over the sides), spreading it in an even layer with the spoon. Return to the freezer until it sets and is no longer sticky, about 1 hour (do not cover).

*5.* Toss all of the peanuts with ½ cup of the peanut butter chips. Sprinkle them in a ring about 1 inch wide around the top edge of the cake. Mound the remaining 2 tablespoons of chips in the center. Refrigerate until ready to serve. Slice the cold cake with a sharp straight-edge knife, not a serrated one. Cover any leftover cake and refrigerate or wrap and freeze for up to 1 month.

### The Junior's Way

Use smooth peanut butter, not chunky, for this cake. We prefer the old-fashioned combination of peanut butter and grape jelly, but strawberry jelly works just as well. Be sure to use jelly, not jam or preserves that contain pieces of fruit.

*You know it's fall when pumpkin cheesecakes start coming out of the ovens at Junior's, and the customers start lining up to pick up their orders. Junior's makes their pumpkin cakes by swirling white and pumpkin batters together, then decorating them with dollops of whipped cream. The result? A dessert that's cheesecake and pumpkin pie, all in one. What a way to celebrate Thanksgiving, or any day!*

# pumpkin swirl cheesecake

**MAKES ONE 9-INCH CHEESECAKE, ABOUT 3 INCHES HIGH**

1 recipe 9-inch Junior's Sponge Cake Crust (page 17)

Four 8-ounce packages cream cheese (use only full fat), at room temperature

1 2/3 cups sugar

1/4 cup cornstarch

1 tablespoon pure vanilla extract

2 extra-large eggs

3/4 cup heavy or whipping cream

1 cup canned pumpkin purée (not pumpkin pie mix)

1 teaspoon pumpkin pie spice, plus more for sprinkling

1 recipe Decorator's Whipped Cream (page 26)

*1.* Preheat the oven to 350°F. Generously butter the bottom and sides of a 9-inch springform pan. Wrap the outside with aluminum foil, covering the bottom and extending all the way up the sides. Make and bake the cake crust and leave in the pan. Keep the oven on.

*2.* Put one package of the cream cheese, 1/3 cup of the sugar, and the cornstarch in a large bowl. Beat with an electric mixer on low until creamy, about 3 minutes, scraping the bowl down several times. Blend in the remaining cream cheese, one package at a time, scraping down the bowl after each one. Increase the mixer speed to medium and beat in the remaining 1 1/3 cups sugar, then the vanilla. Blend in the eggs, one at a time, beating well after adding each one. Beat in the cream just until completely blended. Be careful not to overmix!

*3.* Remove 1 1/2 cups of the batter and set aside. On low speed, blend the pumpkin and the 1 teaspoon of pumpkin pie spice into the remaining batter. Gently spoon the pumpkin batter on top of the crust. Using a teaspoon, drop the white batter in small spoonfuls on top of the pumpkin batter, pushing it down slightly as you go. Using a thin, pointed knife, cut through the batter a few times in a "figure 8" design, just until white swirls appear.

**4.** Place the cake in a large shallow pan containing hot water that comes about 1 inch up the sides of the springform. Bake until the edges are light golden brown and the top has golden and tan swirls, about 1¼ hours. Remove the cheesecake from the water bath, transfer to a wire rack, and let cool for 2 hours (just walk away—don't move it). Leave the cake in the pan, cover loosely with plastic wrap, and refrigerate until completely cold, preferably overnight or at least 4 hours.

**5.** Release and remove the sides of the springform, leaving the cake on the bottom of the pan. Place on a cake plate. Pipe whipped cream rosettes around the top edge of the cake. Lightly sprinkle the cream rosettes (page 26) with a little pumpkin pie spice. Refrigerate until ready to serve. Slice the cold cake with a sharp straight-edge knife, not a serrated one. Cover any leftover cake and refrigerate, or wrap and freeze for up to 1 month.

## The Junior's Way

For this cake, the bakers use canned pumpkin, the kind that's 100 percent pure pumpkin purée, not canned pumpkin pie mix. This works better than cooked fresh pumpkin because the moisture and flavor are consistent, cake after cake.

*Leave it to Junior's to take peanut butter and swirl it into their famous cheesecake, then top it with crushed Heath bars. Go ahead—let them have all they want, whenever they want . . . that's the Junior's way!*

# peanut butter swirl

**MAKES ONE 9-INCH CHEESECAKE, ABOUT 2½ INCHES HIGH**

1 recipe 9-inch Junior's
Sponge Cake Crust (page 17)

Three 8-ounce packages
cream cheese (use only full fat),
at room temperature

1⅓ cups sugar

3 tablespoons cornstarch

1 tablespoon pure vanilla extract

2 extra-large eggs

⅔ cup plus ½ cup
heavy or whipping cream

2 cups smooth peanut butter

Five 1.4-ounce Heath®
milk chocolate English toffee
candy bars

¼ cup lightly salted
dry-roasted peanuts

*1.* Preheat the oven to 350°F. Generously butter the bottom and sides of a 9-inch springform pan. Wrap the outside with aluminum foil, covering the bottom and extending all the way up the sides. Make and bake the cake crust and leave it in the pan. Keep the oven on.

*2.* Put one package of the cream cheese, ⅓ cup of the sugar, and the cornstarch in a large bowl. Beat with an electric mixer on low until creamy, about 3 minutes, scraping the bowl down several times. Blend in the remaining cream cheese, one package at a time, scraping down the bowl after each one. Increase the mixer speed to medium and beat in the remaining 1 cup sugar, then the vanilla. Blend in the eggs, one at a time, beating well after adding each one. Beat in the ⅔ cup of the heavy cream just until completely blended. Be careful not to overmix! Gently spoon the batter on top of the crust.

*3.* Mix together the peanut butter and remaining ½ cup heavy cream in a medium-size bowl until smooth. Using a teaspoon, drop the peanut butter in small spoonfuls on top of the batter in the pan, pushing it down slightly into the filling as you go. Using a thin, pointed knife, cut through the batter a few times in a "figure 8" design, just until golden-brown swirls appear.

*4.* Place the cake in a large shallow pan containing hot water that comes about 1 inch up the sides of the springform. Bake until the edges are light golden brown and the top has golden and tan swirls, about 1¼ hours. Remove the cheesecake from the water bath, transfer to a wire rack, and let cool for 2 hours (just walk away—don't move it). Leave the cake in the pan, cover loosely with plastic wrap, and refrigerate until completely cold, preferably overnight or at least 4 hours.

*5.* While the cake chills, cut 1 Heath bar into 2 equal pieces and reserve for the center decoration. Chop the remaining 4 bars with a chef's knife into chunky, coarse pieces.

*6.* To decorate the cake, release and remove the sides of the springform, leaving the cake on the bottom of the pan. Place on a cake plate and sprinkle with the Heath bar pieces. Decorate the center with the 2 large pieces and the peanuts. Refrigerate until ready to serve. Slice with a sharp straight-edge knife, not a serrated one. Cover any leftover cake and refrigerate, or wrap and freeze for up to 1 month.

## The Junior's Way

Thin the peanut butter with the cream after the cheesecake batter is in the pan, then swirl into the filling right away. If the peanut butter is allowed to stand, it will thicken up and be difficult to work into the batter.

# Cheesecakes with Fruit

Many folks who come to Junior's want their cheesecake plain — no topping, no swirls, nothing extra — just plain vanilla. But Junior's does take many of their cakes a step or two further, such as swirling in a fruit purée or baking a fresh apple pie filling inside. "We also use a lot of fruits to decorate our cheesecakes," says Alan Rosen, "because they're a quick and easy way to add that special Junior's touch, without much effort." The possibilities of combining fruits with Junior's cheesecakes to create exciting new taste sensations are endless.

*Junior's has created this delicious cake by flavoring their original cheesecake filling with plenty of white chocolate, then swirling in raspberry purée. Crown it with a pinwheel of fresh raspberries and curls of white chocolate. It's ready to impress anyone lucky enough to get a slice!*

# white chocolate & raspberry swirl

MAKES ONE 9-INCH CHEESECAKE, ABOUT 3 INCHES HIGH

1 recipe 9-inch Junior's
Sponge Cake Crust (page 17)

10 ounces dry-pack
frozen whole raspberries
(unsweetened, not in syrup),
thawed and drained well

5 tablespoons cornstarch

8 ounces white chocolate

Three 8-ounce packages
cream cheese (use only full fat),
at room temperature

1 1/3 cups sugar

1 tablespoon pure vanilla extract

2 extra-large eggs

2/3 cup heavy or whipping cream

1 half-pint fresh raspberries
(about 6 ounces)

White chocolate curls
(page 21)

*1.* Preheat the oven to 350°F. Generously butter the bottom and sides of a 9-inch springform pan. Wrap the outside with aluminum foil, covering the bottom and extending all the way up the sides. Make and bake the cake crust and leave it in the pan. Keep the oven on.

*2.* Pulse the thawed raspberries in your food processor until puréed (you need 3/4 cup of purée). Stir in 1 tablespoon of the cornstarch and set aside. It will thicken slightly as it stands. Melt the white chocolate (see The Junior's Way on page 58) and set aside.

*3.* Put one package of the cream cheese, 1/3 cup of the sugar, and the remaining 4 tablespoons of cornstarch in a large bowl. Beat with an electric mixer on low until creamy, about 3 minutes, scraping down the bowl several times. Beat in the remaining cream cheese, one package at a time, scraping down the bowl after each one. Increase the mixer speed to medium and beat in the remaining 1 cup sugar, then the vanilla. Blend in the eggs, one at a time, beating well after adding each one. Beat in the melted white chocolate, then the cream, just until completely blended. Be careful not to overmix!

*4.* Gently spoon the batter on top of the crust. Using a teaspoon, drop the raspberry purée in spoonfuls on top of the batter, pushing it down slightly as you go. Using a thin, pointed knife, cut through the batter a few times in a

"figure 8" design, just until red swirls appear (don't mix in the purée completely or the cake will turn pink).

5. Place the cake in a large shallow pan containing hot water that comes about 1 inch up the sides of the springform. Bake until the edges are light golden brown and the top is slightly golden tan with red raspberry swirls, about 1¼ hours. Remove the cheesecake from the water bath, transfer to a wire rack, and let cool for 2 hours (just walk away—don't move it!). Leave the cake in the pan, cover with plastic wrap, and refrigerate until completely cold, preferably overnight or at least 4 hours.

6. To decorate, release and remove the sides of the springform, leaving the cake on the bottom of the pan. Place on a cake plate. Decorate the top with a pinwheel of raspberries, standing the berries with their points up and mounding a few extra berries in the center. Shower the top with white chocolate curls. Refrigerate until ready to serve. Cover any leftover cake and refrigerate, or remove the fresh berries, then wrap and freeze for up to 1 month.

*The Junior's Way*

White chocolate is so delicate that it scorches very easily. Melt it in a small saucepan over very low heat, stirring it constantly. Or, microwave it uncovered, on high, for 30 seconds. Stir with a dry spoon, then repeat 2 to 3 times (8 ounces of white chocolate will melt in about 1½ minutes). Watch closely! The chocolate bars keep their shape so they might look like they need more heating, when they are actually already completely melted. Too much heat can curdle and ruin this chocolate.

*This cake is so pretty and makes such an impression that you can serve it with no further embellishment, or you can dress it up for a party with rows and rows of fresh fruits.*

# raspberry swirl cheesecake

**ONE 9-INCH CHEESECAKE, ABOUT 3 INCHES HIGH**

1 recipe 9-inch Junior's Sponge Cake Crust (page 17)

10 ounces (about 1 cup) dry-pack frozen whole raspberries (unsweetened, not in syrup), thawed and drained well

¼ cup plus 1 teaspoon cornstarch

Three 8-ounce packages cream cheese (use only full fat), at room temperature

1⅓ cups sugar

1 tablespoon pure vanilla extract

2 extra-large eggs

⅔ cup heavy or whipping cream, plus 1 tablespoon for brushing

1 quart ripe strawberries, hulled and cut vertically into ¼-inch-thick slices

1 half-pint fresh blackberries (about 6 ounces)

1 half-pint fresh raspberries (about 6 ounces)

*1.* Preheat the oven to 350°F. Generously butter the bottom and sides of a 9-inch springform pan. Wrap the outside with aluminum foil, covering the bottom and extending all the way up the sides. Make and bake the cake crust and leave it in the pan. Keep the oven on.

*2.* Pulse the thawed raspberries in a food processor until puréed (you need ¾ cup of purée). Stir in the 1 teaspoon of cornstarch and set aside. It will thicken slightly as it stands.

*3.* Put one package of the cream cheese, ⅓ cup of the sugar, and the remaining ¼ cup cornstarch in a large bowl. Beat with an electric mixer on low until creamy, about 3 minutes, scraping down the bowl several times. Beat in the remaining cream cheese, one package at a time, scraping down the bowl after each one. Increase the mixer speed to medium and beat in the remaining 1 cup sugar, then the vanilla. Blend in the eggs, one at a time, beating well after adding each one. Beat in the ⅔ cup cream just until completely blended. Be careful not to overmix! Gently spoon the batter on top of the crust.

*4.* Using a teaspoon, drop the raspberry purée in small spoonfuls on top of the batter, pushing it down slightly as you go. Using a thin, pointed knife, cut through the batter a few times in a "figure 8" design, just until red swirls appear (do not mix in the purée completely or the cake will turn pink).

*5.* Place the cake in a large shallow pan containing hot water that comes about 1 inch up the sides of the springform. Bake until the edges are light golden brown and the top of the cake is slightly golden tan with red raspberry swirls, about 1¼ hours. Remove the cheesecake from the water bath, transfer to a wire rack, and let cool for 2 hours (just walk away—don't move it). Cover the cake with plastic wrap and refrigerate until completely cold, preferably overnight or at least 4 hours.

*6.* To decorate, release and remove the sides of the springform, leaving the cake on the bottom of the pan. Place on a cake plate. Brush the top with the remaining 1 tablespoon cream. Cover the top with the berries, arranging them in alternating rows. Refrigerate until ready to serve. Cover any leftover cake and store in the refrigerator, or remove the fresh berries, then wrap and freeze up to 1 month.

## The Junior's Way

When using fresh berries to decorate cakes, wash them thoroughly, then dry on paper towels. Don't skip the drying step, as it helps prevent the berries from discoloring the white cheesecake filling. Arrange the different kinds in alternating rows on top of the cold cake (if the cake is still warm, the berries will soften and not look fresh for long). Master Baker Michael Goodman advises: "Do not glaze or sweeten the berries, as this softens and wilts them, causing them to lose their shape."

*This cake gets its name from the tall ice cream parfaits served at the soda fountain. Just like in those ice cream creations, the bakers make this cheesecake in layers. They use a pink strawberry cheesecake batter for the bottom layer, then stir bits of strawberries into the white batter for the top layer. The crowning touch is one of Junior's specialties—a glossy red "mirror" made of strawberry jelly. This is as good, and as pretty, as it gets!*

# strawberry parfait

**MAKES ONE 9-INCH CHEESECAKE, ABOUT 3 INCHES HIGH**

1 recipe 9-inch Junior's
Sponge Cake Crust (page 17)

**FOR THE STRAWBERRY
CHEESECAKE LAYERS:**

10 ounces (about 1 cup)
dry-pack frozen whole strawberries
(unsweetened, not in syrup),
thawed and drained

1/3 cup plus 1 teaspoon cornstarch

Three 8-ounce packages
cream cheese (use only full fat),
at room temperature

1 1/3 cups sugar

1 tablespoon pure vanilla extract

2 extra-large eggs

2/3 cup heavy or whipping cream

3 to 4 drops red food coloring

1 quart ripe fresh strawberries,
hulled

**FOR THE RED MIRROR:**

1/2 cup strawberry jelly
(not preserves or jam)

1 teaspoon light corn syrup

2 to 3 drops red food coloring

*1.* Preheat the oven to 350°F. Generously butter the bottom and sides of a 9-inch springform pan. Wrap the outside with aluminum foil, covering the bottom and extending all the way up the sides. Make and bake the cake crust and leave it in the pan. Keep the oven on.

*2.* Pulse the thawed strawberries in your food processor until smooth (you need 3/4 cup of purée). Stir in the 1 teaspoon of cornstarch and set aside. It will thicken slightly as it stands.

*3.* Put one package of the cream cheese, 1/3 cup of the sugar, and the remaining 1/3 cup cornstarch in a large bowl. Beat with an electric mixer on low until creamy, about 3 minutes, scraping down the bowl a few times. Beat in the remaining cream cheese, one package at a time, scraping down the bowl after each one. Increase the mixer speed to medium and beat in the remaining 1 cup sugar, then the vanilla. Beat in the eggs, one at a time, blending well after adding each one. Beat in the cream just until completely blended. Be careful not to overmix.

*4.* Divide the cheesecake filling into two equal parts. Blend the strawberry purée and red food coloring into one half of the batter, using just enough food coloring to turn the batter a light pink (no more!). Spoon into the crust and spread out evenly.

*5.* Coarsely chop half of the fresh berries (you need 1 cup). Fold them into the remaining filling and gently spread over the pink layer, pushing it out to the sides of the pan. For the top decoration, cut the remaining berries vertically (from top to tip) into ¼-inch-thick slices and refrigerate.

*6.* Place the cake in a large shallow pan containing hot water that comes about 1 inch up the sides of the springform. Bake until the edges are light golden brown and the top is set, about 1¼ hours. Remove the cheesecake from the water bath, transfer to a wire rack, and let cool for 2 hours (just walk away—don't move it). Loosely cover the cake (still in the pan) with plastic wrap and refrigerate until completely cold, preferably overnight or at least 4 hours. Transfer to the freezer for 1 hour.

*7.* To make the red mirror, put the jelly and corn syrup in a small saucepan and stir constantly over low heat just until melted (do not let it boil!). Remove from the heat and add the red food coloring. Spoon the jelly evenly over the top of the cake and return to the freezer for about 30 minutes, until set (do not cover).

*8.* To serve, release and remove the sides of the springform, leaving the cake on the bottom of the pan. Place on a cake plate. Decorate the rim of the cake with the sliced berries, arranging the pointed ends of the berries out to the edge. Refrigerate until ready to serve. Slice with a sharp straight-edge knife, not a serrated one. Refrigerate any leftover cake or remove the fresh berries, then wrap and freeze for up to 1 month.

*The Junior's Way*

Before making the red mirror, chill the cake (still in the pan) in the freezer for 1 hour until very cold. Spoon on the melted jelly, then return the cake to the freezer for about 30 minutes to set the mirror before removing the cake from the pan.

*Here's Junior's answer to those popular fruit tarts found in many pastry shops and upscale restaurants. The bakers use that same famous cheesecake filling, just less of it, and they use the best berries in the market that day. Any combination works. Just be sure to leave some of the creamy cheesecake filling showing on top, like they do at Junior's.*

# junior's cheesecake tart

**MAKES ONE 11- OR 12-INCH CHEESECAKE TART**

1 recipe 11- or 12-inch
All-Butter Tart Crust (page 19)

Two 8-ounce packages
cream cheese (use only full fat),
at room temperature

$2/3$ cup sugar

2 tablespoons cornstarch

2 teaspoons pure vanilla extract

1 extra-large egg

$1/2$ cup heavy or whipping cream

1 pint ripe strawberries

1 pint fresh blackberries
(about 12 ounces)

1 half-pint fresh raspberries
(about 6 ounces)

Fresh mint leaves

*1.* Preheat the oven to 350°F. Generously butter the bottom and sides of an 11- or 12-inch tart pan (a nonstick one with a removable bottom and 1-inch sides). Wrap the outside with aluminum foil, covering the bottom and extending all the way up the sides. Make and bake the tart crust and leave it in the pan. Keep the oven on.

*2.* Put one package of the cream cheese, $1/3$ cup of the sugar, and the cornstarch in a large bowl. Beat with an electric mixer on low until creamy, about 3 minutes (be sure to scrape down the bowl a few times). Beat in the remaining package of cream cheese. Increase the mixer speed to medium and beat in the remaining $1/3$ cup sugar, then the vanilla. Blend in the egg, then the cream, beating just until completely blended. Be careful not to overmix! Gently spoon the batter into the tart shell.

*3.* Place the tart in a large shallow pan containing hot water that comes only about halfway up the sides of the tart pan (no higher). Bake until the edges of the crust are light golden brown and the center is set and light gold, about 30 minutes. Remove the cheesecake from the water bath, transfer to a wire rack, and let cool for 2 hours (just walk away—don't move it). Leave the tart in the pan, cover loosely with plastic wrap, and refrigerate until completely cold, preferably overnight or at least 4 hours.

*4.* To decorate, remove the ring of the pan. Slide the tart off the bottom of the pan onto a cake plate (or leave the tart on the bottom of the pan and place right on the plate).

*5.* Wash the berries and dry on paper towels (very important!). Pick out 12 strawberries of similar size. Hull, then cut them in half vertically from top to tip. Halve the blackberries the same way. Arrange the strawberries in a circle around the edge of the tart with tips pointing out. Follow with 2 circles of blackberries, angling them and resting the tips of the berries on adjacent berries so they stand up slightly. Stand up a cluster of raspberries in the center with tips pointing up. Top with a few mint leaves. Refrigerate until ready to serve. Cover any leftovers and refrigerate (do not freeze).

## The Junior's Way

After baking the crust, let it cool for a few minutes. Then pat it down gently with your fingers to burst any little bubbles. This gives plenty of space to put in the filling.

*As the story goes, the first Key lime pie dates back to the early 1900s or before. Junior's begins their lime dessert with a layer of their original cheesecake. Then they spoon on a mound of whipped cream lime mousse and shower it with lots of graham cracker crumbs. They finish it off by piping even more lime mousse on top and decorating with green sugary candies.*

# key lime mousse cheesecake

1 recipe 9-inch Junior's
Shortbread Crust (page 18)

**FOR THE CHEESECAKE:**
Three 8-ounce packages
cream cheese (use only full fat),
at room temperature

1⅓ cups sugar

3 tablespoons cornstarch

1 tablespoon pure vanilla extract

2 extra-large eggs

⅔ cup heavy or whipping cream

**FOR THE LIME MOUSSE:**
1 tablespoon unflavored
granulated gelatin

2 tablespoons cold water

4 large cinnamon graham crackers

3 cups heavy or whipping cream

2 tablespoons sugar

¾ cup frozen limeade concentrate
(6 ounces)

1 to 2 drops of green food coloring
(optional)

**FOR THE DECORATION:**
8 sugared "spearmint leaf"
gumdrops, cut in half horizontally

**MAKES ONE 9-INCH CHEESECAKE, ABOUT 3 INCHES HIGH**

*1.* Preheat the oven to 350°F. Generously butter the bottom and sides of a 9-inch springform pan. Wrap the outside with aluminum foil, covering the bottom and extending all the way up the sides. Make and bake the shortcake crust and leave it in the pan. Keep the oven on.

*2.* Put one package of the cream cheese, ⅓ cup of the sugar, and the cornstarch in a large bowl. Beat with an electric mixer on low until creamy, about 3 minutes, scraping down the bowl several times. Beat in the remaining cream cheese, one package at a time, scraping down the bowl after each one. Increase the mixer speed to medium and beat in the remaining 1 cup sugar, then the vanilla. Blend in the eggs, one at a time, beating well after adding each one. Beat in the cream just until completely blended. Be careful not to overmix! Gently spoon the batter on top of the baked crust.

*3.* Place the cake in a large shallow pan containing hot water that comes about 1 inch up the sides of the springform. Bake until the edges are light golden brown and the top is slightly golden tan, about 1¼ hours. Remove the cheesecake from the water bath, transfer to a wire rack, and let cool for 2 hours (just walk away—don't move it). Leave the cake in the pan, cover loosely with plastic wrap, and refrigerate until thoroughly chilled, about 4 hours.

*4.* Meanwhile, make the lime mousse. Place the gelatin in a heatproof measuring cup, stir in the cold water and let stand until thickened. Cook in the microwave on high for about 30 seconds or place over a pan of simmering water for about 1 minute, until completely melted. Set aside to cool. Process the graham crackers in a food processor until crumbs form (you need ½ cup).

*5.* In a large bowl, whip the cream with the mixer on high just until it thickens and peaks begin to form. With the mixer still running, add the sugar. Blend in the limeade concentrate (do not dilute!) and a couple of drops of green food coloring if you wish. Beat in the dissolved gelatin all at once, just until it disappears. Watch carefully and do not overbeat at this stage. Refrigerate until ready to use. It's best if the mousse is spooned and piped onto the cheesecake right away.

*6.* Remove the cold cake from the refrigerator. Scoop out 1½ cups of the lime mousse into a small bowl to use for the rosettes and return to the refrigerator. Spoon the remaining lime mousse on top of the cake (still in the pan). Smooth out with a metal spatula, pushing it out to the sides of the pan. Sprinkle the top evenly with the graham cracker crumbs. Fit a pastry bag with a medium open-star tip and fill with the 1½ cups reserved lime mousse. Pipe 12 to 14 rosettes (page 26) around the top rim of the cake. Place the cake in the freezer, uncovered, until the mousse is firm and set, about 4 hours or overnight (do not cover). If you're not serving the cake the same day, loosely cover with plastic wrap after the rosettes have frozen and return the cake to the freezer.

*7.* About 2 hours before serving, let the cake stand at room temperature for about 15 minutes, just long enough to release the sides of the springform. Transfer to a cake plate, leaving the cake on the bottom of the pan. Decorate each rosette with half of a sugared candy. Refrigerate the cake (do not cover) until time to serve (it'll take about 2 hours to thaw in the refrigerator so you can slice it easily). Refrigerate any leftover cake or wrap and return to the freezer for up to 1 month.

*The Junior's Way*

It would take bushels of limes and a lot of bakers to squeeze enough of them to make hundreds of these lime mousse cakes. So Junior's uses fresh frozen lime juice to get the same fabulous taste with a lot less effort. "You can't buy frozen lime juice in your supermarket easily but the frozen limeade concentrate works just as well," says Junior's Master Baker Michael Goodman.

*Remember those caramel apples on a stick sold at the state fairs and the farmers' markets? Here is Junior's creation of that wonderful combination. Start with Junior's original cheesecake batter and top with a fresh apple pie filling. As the cake bakes, the apples form a golden-brown topping with just enough crispness and crunch to contrast perfectly with the soft creaminess of the cheesecake. Drizzle the cake generously with a delicious caramel topping and add more fresh apples for that impressive finishing touch, the Junior's way!*

# apple caramel cheesecake

1 recipe 9-inch Junior's
Sponge Cake Crust (page 17)

**FOR THE APPLE FILLING:**

3 large firm, crisp red-skinned
apples

½ cup apple cider or apple juice

1 tablespoon cornstarch

1 tablespoon sugar

¼ teaspoon ground cinnamon

**FOR THE CHEESECAKE:**

Three 8-ounce packages
cream cheese (use only full fat),
at room temperature

1⅓ cups sugar

¼ cup cornstarch

1 tablespoon pure vanilla extract

2 extra-large eggs

⅔ cup heavy or whipping cream

**FOR THE APPLE CARAMEL
TOPPING:**

2 large firm, crisp red-skinned
apples

Juice of 1 large lemon

1 cup caramel or butterscotch
ice cream topping

**MAKES ONE 9-INCH CHEESECAKE, ABOUT 3 INCHES HIGH**

*1.* Preheat the oven to 350°F. Generously butter the bottom and sides of a 9-inch springform pan. Wrap the outside with aluminum foil, covering the bottom and extending all the way up the sides. Make and bake the cake crust and leave it in the pan. Keep the oven on.

*2.* To make the filling, peel and core the apples for the filling into ½-inch, bite-size pieces. Combine the cider, cornstarch, sugar, and cinnamon in a small saucepan and whisk until completely dissolved. While stirring constantly, bring to a full boil over medium heat and continue to boil until thickened, about 2 minutes. Remove from the heat and stir in the apples. Set aside to cool while you make the cake.

*3.* Put one package of the cream cheese, ⅓ cup of the sugar, and the corn-starch in a large bowl. Beat with an electric mixer on low until creamy, about 3 minutes, scraping the bowl down several times. Blend in the remaining cream cheese, one package at a time, scraping down the bowl after each one. Increase the mixer speed to medium and beat in the remaining 1 cup sugar, then the vanilla. Blend in the eggs, one at a time, beating well after adding each one. Beat in the cream just until completely blended. Be careful not to overmix! Gently

spoon the batter on top of the crust, then spoon the apple mixture over the batter, gently spreading it almost to the edge of the pan, completely covering the cake.

*4.* Place the cake in a large shallow pan containing hot water that comes about 1 inch up the sides of the springform. Bake until the edges are light golden brown and the top is slightly golden tan, about 1¼ hours. Remove the cheesecake from the water bath, transfer to a wire rack, and let cool for 2 hours (just walk away—don't move it). Leave the cake in the pan, cover loosely with plastic wrap, and refrigerate until completely cold, preferably overnight or at least 4 hours. Transfer the cake to the freezer for 1 hour.

*5.* For the prettiest cake, decorate within a few hours before serving, so the apples stay fresh and crisp. To make the topping, core the apples and thinly slice them or cut them into bite-size pieces (leave the peel on if you like). Toss the apples with the lemon juice (this keeps them from turning brown). Release and remove the sides of the springform, leaving the cake on the bottom of the pan. Place on a serving plate. Top the cake with the apples (wipe them with a paper towel first).

*6.* Warm the caramel ice cream topping (don't let it boil), then drizzle it from the tip of a small spoon in stripes across the top of the cake, all around the edges, and some down the sides. Return the cake to the freezer until the caramel has set, 30 minutes. Refrigerate the cake until ready to serve. Slice with a sharp straight-edge knife, not a serrated one. Cover any leftover cake and refrigerate. Do not freeze this cake.

*The Junior's Way*

Buy firm, crisp, juicy, sweet all-purpose apples, such as Gala, Jonathan, or McIntosh. The apples for the filling are cut into bite-size pieces. When cut this size, they bake just until tender, yet still hold their shape. And they're small enough to not interfere with cutting the slices of cake. Before decorating with the caramel topping, freeze the cake for an hour until the top and sides are set and very cold. As you drizzle on the caramel, it will stay exactly where you want it, not in a pool on the plate.

*Before Junior's, Harry Rosen had the Enduro Sandwich Shops, where there was usually a homemade pie coming out of the oven at any hour. Chances were on most days, it would be cherry. These days, you can find that same cherry pie filling baked inside a Junior's cheesecake and topped with buttery cinnamon crumbs.*

# cherry crumb cheesecake

**MAKES ONE 9-INCH CHEESECAKE, ABOUT 3 INCHES HIGH**

1 recipe 9-inch Junior's Sponge Cake Crust (page 17)

**FOR THE CHERRY FILLING:**

One 24-ounce jar pitted red sour cherries in juice (fresh-frozen and thawed, or canned)

2 tablespoons cornstarch

2 tablespoons sugar

2 teaspoons fresh lemon juice

Red food coloring (optional)

**FOR THE CHEESECAKE:**

Three 8-ounce packages cream cheese (use only full fat), at room temperature

1 1/3 cups sugar

1/4 cup cornstarch

1 tablespoon pure vanilla extract

2 extra-large eggs

2/3 cup heavy or whipping cream

**FOR THE TOPPING:**

1 recipe Junior's Cinnamon Crumb Topping (page 29)

*1.* Preheat the oven to 350°F. Generously butter the bottom and sides of a 9-inch springform pan. Wrap the outside with aluminum foil, covering the bottom and extending all the way up the sides. Make and bake the cake crust and leave it in the pan. Keep the oven on.

*2.* To make the filling, drain the cherries, reserving 1 cup of the juice (if necessary, add water to make 1 cup). Refrigerate 7 cherries for decorating the cake. Stir the cornstarch into the juice in a small saucepan until completely dissolved, then stir in the sugar. Bring to a full boil over medium heat. Cook and stir constantly until the mixture turns clear and thickens (very important!), about 2 minutes. Remove from the heat and stir in the lemon juice and food coloring, if you wish. Fold in the cherries. Let cool while you make the cheesecake batter.

*3.* Put one package of the cream cheese, 1/3 cup of the sugar, and the cornstarch in a large bowl. Beat with an electric mixer on low until creamy, about 3 minutes, scraping down the bowl several times. Beat in the remaining cream cheese, one package at a time, scraping down the bowl after each one. Increase the mixer speed to medium and beat in the remaining 1 cup sugar, then the vanilla. Blend in the eggs, one at a time, beating well after adding each one. Beat in the cream just until completely blended. Be careful not to overmix! Spread half the cherry mixture over the crust. Gently spoon the cheesecake

spoon the batter into the pan, then spoon the peach mixture on top. Gently spread the peaches almost to the edge of the pan, covering the filling.

*4.* Place the cake in a large shallow pan containing hot water that comes about 1 inch up the sides of the springform. Bake until the edges are light golden brown and the top is slightly golden tan, about 1¼ hours. Remove the cheesecake from the water bath, transfer to a wire rack, and let cool for 2 hours (just walk away—don't move it). Leave the cake in the pan, cover loosely with plastic wrap, and refrigerate until completely cold, preferably overnight or at least 4 hours.

*5.* Make and bake the crumb topping. To decorate, release and remove the sides of the springform, leaving the cake on the bottom of the pan. Place on a serving plate. Top the cake with the cinnamon crumbs and decorate the center with the reserved peach slices. Refrigerate until ready to serve. Slice with a sharp straight-edge knife, not a serrated one. Cover any leftover cake and refrigerate or freeze for up to 1 month.

## The Junior's Way

Look for frozen dry-packed peaches for this cake; they're so much easier to use than starting with fresh fruit. Cut them into bite-size pieces; that'll make the cake much easier to slice.

# Celebration Cheesecakes

There's always a celebration going on at Junior's! If it's Easter, there are often egg-shaped cheesecakes with pastel flowers; in the summertime, you're likely to see cheesecakes decorated with Ol' Glory; and in December, ones that are laden with cranberry swirls, in the spirit of Christmas. But even if it's not holiday time, there's always someone who wants to toast an anniversary, rejoice over a graduation, enjoy a birthday, or entertain friends. Now you can celebrate those times with a fabulous Junior's cheesecake that you've baked yourself. Try an impressive Tiramisu Cake that's wrapped in ladyfingers and topped with mascarpone cream. Whatever you fancy, these cakes are guaranteed to impress!

*Nothing says "I love you" more than lots of hearts—and they seem to be everywhere at Junior's several weeks before Valentine's Day. There are heart-shaped cookies with lacy decorations, and, of course, delicious cheesecakes in the shape of valentines. This recipe is Junior's favorite, with dark sweet cherry purée swirled throughout, plus rosettes of whipped cream piped all around and cherry preserves in the shape of a heart in the center of it all. It's the perfect cake to bake for your sweetheart!*

*You'll need a deep 10-cup heart-shaped "molded" cake pan with heart designs on the sides to make this cake (usually called a deep crown of heart pan), or a plain 9-cup heart pan, which you can find at gourmet and bakeware sites on the Internet and in specialty cookware stores, especially around Valentine's Day. We've skipped the crust in this recipe, so the cheesecake batter takes on all of the fancy patterns of the mold during baking.*

# cherry heart cheesecake

**MAKES ONE 11-INCH HEART-SHAPED CHEESECAKE. TO USE A STRAIGHT-SIDED HEART PAN WITH A SMALLER CAPACITY, FOLLOW THE DIRECTIONS IN OUR VARIATION.**

10 ounces (about 1 cup) dry-pack frozen pitted Bing cherries (not in syrup), thawed and drained well

5 tablespoons cornstarch

Four 8-ounce packages cream cheese (use only full fat), at room temperature

1²/₃ cups sugar

1 tablespoon pure vanilla extract

2 extra-large eggs

³/₄ cup heavy or whipping cream

1 recipe Decorator's Whipped Cream (page 26)

¹/₂ cup cherry preserves (with whole cherries)

*1.* Preheat the oven to 350°F. Generously butter the bottom and sides of a deep 10-cup heart-shaped mold (about 11 inches wide, 10 inches long, 2½ inches high). Line the pan with two pieces of aluminum foil, crisscrossing them and leaving a 3-inch overhang all around. Press the foil gently but firmly into the mold, shaping it into all of its curves so the baked cake will have all of the details of the heart mold (be careful to not tear the foil). There's no need to wrap the outside of the pan. Butter the foil.

*2.* Pulse the thawed cherries in your food processor until smooth (you need ³/₄ cup of purée). Stir in 1 tablespoon of the cornstarch and set aside. It will thicken slightly as it stands.

*3.* Put one package of the cream cheese, ¹/₃ cup of the sugar, and the remaining 4 tablespoons cornstarch in a large bowl and beat with an electric mixer on low until creamy, about 3 minutes, scraping down the bowl a couple of times. Blend

in the remaining cream cheese, one package at a time, scraping down the bowl after each one. Increase the mixer speed to medium and beat in the remaining 1⅓ cups sugar, then the vanilla. Blend in the eggs, one at a time, beating well after adding each one. Beat in the cream just until completely blended. Be careful not to overmix!

*4.* Spread half the cheese filling in the heart pan. Using a teaspoon, drop the purée in small spoonfuls on top of the batter, pushing it down slightly as you go. Using a thin, pointed knife, cut through the batter a few times in a "figure 8" design, just until red swirls appear (don't mix in the purée completely or the whole cake will turn purple and you'll lose the swirls). Gently and carefully, spread the remaining cheese filling on top, trying not to move the swirls. (This will let the cherry swirls show through when the cake is turned upside down onto a serving platter.)

*5.* Place in a large shallow pan containing hot water that comes about 1 inch up the sides of the heart pan. Bake until the edges are light golden brown and the top is slightly golden tan, about 1¼ hours. Remove the cheesecake from the water bath, transfer to a wire rack, and let cool for 2 hours (just walk away— don't move it). Cover with plastic wrap and refrigerate until completely cold, at least 4 hours. Transfer to the freezer until frozen solid, preferably overnight, or at least 4 hours.

*6.* To decorate, first remove the cake from the freezer and let it stand at room temperature while you make the whipped cream. Put the cream in the refrigerator to chill for 30 minutes. Meanwhile, remove the cake from the pan by turning it upside down onto a cake plate or platter without a rim and gently peel off the foil. If the cake does not release easily from the pan, place it on a burner over low heat for about 10 seconds, just long enough to melt the butter greasing the pan (use potholders!).

*7.* Fit a pastry bag with a closed-star tip (#31) or medium open-star tip (#32), fill with some of the whipped cream, and pipe rosettes (page 26) around the bottom edge of the cake. Use a small open-star tip (#17) to pipe a heart in the center of the cake. Fill the heart with the preserves.

*8.* Refrigerate until ready to serve. Slice with a sharp straight-edge knife, not a serrated one. Cover any leftover cake and refrigerate, or wrap and freeze for up to 1 month.

**FOR A 9-INCH (9-CUP) HEART PAN:**
Choose a deep, straight-sided heart-shaped cake pan, 9 inches long and at least 2 inches deep, that holds 8 cups of batter. Use 8 ounces of drained cherries (½ cup purée), 4 tablespoons cornstarch, three 8-ounce packages cream cheese, 1⅓ cups sugar, 1 tablespoon vanilla, 2 extra-large eggs, and ⅔ cup heavy cream and follow the directions above.

*The Junior's Way*

This cake needs to be frozen in order to remove it easily from the mold. Once it's frozen, you can decorate it whenever you like and refrigerate it until serving time. Just be sure to do this at least 2 hours before you plan to serve, to give the cake time to thaw and make it easy to slice.

*Stir chocolate chips into Junior's plain cheesecake batter and lace it with crème de menthe. Bake and chill and it's ready for any celebration. Thanks to the green swirls of crème de menthe, this dessert practically decorates itself. Serve this cake for a St. Patrick's Day party, a spring patio supper, or a Christmas holiday gathering.*

# crème de menthe cheesecake

**MAKES ONE 9-INCH CHEESECAKE, ABOUT 2½ INCHES HIGH**

1 recipe 9-inch Junior's Sponge Cake Crust (page 17)

Four 8-ounce packages cream cheese (use only full fat), at room temperature

1⅔ cups sugar

¼ cup plus 1 teaspoon cornstarch

1 tablespoon pure vanilla extract

2 extra-large eggs

¾ cup heavy or whipping cream

1 tablespoon green crème de menthe liqueur

¾ cup mini chocolate chips

1 recipe Decorator's Whipped Cream (page 26)

8 chocolate-covered mints (1½ inches in diameter)

*1.* Preheat the oven to 350°F. Generously butter the bottom and sides of a 9-inch springform pan. Wrap the outside with aluminum foil, covering the bottom and extending all the way up the sides. Make and bake the sponge cake crust and leave it in the pan. Keep the oven on.

*2.* Put one package of the cream cheese, ⅓ cup of the sugar, and the ¼ cup of cornstarch in a large bowl and beat with an electric mixer on low until creamy, about 3 minutes, scraping down the bowl a couple of times. Blend in the remaining cream cheese, one package at a time, scraping down the bowl after each one. Increase the mixer speed to medium and beat in the remaining 1⅓ cups sugar, then the vanilla. Blend in the eggs, one at a time, beating well after adding each one. Beat in the cream only until completely blended. Be careful not to overmix! Measure out 1 cup of the batter into a measuring cup and stir in the crème de menthe and the remaining 1 teaspoon cornstarch until the batter turns light green. Set aside. Fold the chocolate chips into the remaining batter in the large bowl and gently spoon over the crust.

*3.* Using a teaspoon, drop the green crème de menthe batter in small spoonfuls on top of the batter, pushing it down slightly as you go. Using a thin, pointed knife, cut through the batter a few times in a "figure 8" design, just until green swirls appear (do not swirl too much or the whole cake will turn green and you'll lose the swirls).

*4.* Place in a large shallow pan containing hot water that comes about 1 inch up the sides of the springform. Bake until the edges are light golden brown and the top is slightly golden tan, about 1¼ hours. Remove the cake from the water bath, transfer to a wire rack, and let cool for 2 hours (just walk away—don't move it). Cover with plastic wrap and refrigerate until completely cold, preferably overnight or for at least 4 hours. Transfer to the freezer for at least 2 hours or until ready to decorate the cake (the frosting will set faster and be easier to handle on the cold slightly frozen cake).

*5.* To decorate, release and remove the sides of the springform, leaving the cake on the bottom of the pan. Place on a cake plate. Transfer about half the whipped cream to a separate small bowl and refrigerate. Using a long metal icing spatula, frost the sides of the cake with the remaining frosting, smoothing it flat to give that professional look. (Leave the top unfrosted so the green swirls show.) Fit a pastry bag with a medium closed-star tip (#35) or a medium open-star tip (#32) and fill with some of the reserved frosting. Pipe rosettes (page 26) around the top edge of the cake. Cut 7 of the mints in half and stand them up, cut side down, between the rosettes. Pipe a large rosette in the center and place the whole mint on top. Refrigerate until ready to serve. Slice with a sharp straight-edge knife, not a serrated one. Cover any leftover cake and refrigerate, or wrap and freeze for up to 1 month.

## The Junior's Way

If you can only find clear crème de menthe, use it, but tint it with a few drops of green food coloring until you get a bright green color.

*Leave it to Junior's to turn a cheesecake into an Easter egg! They bake their famous cheesecake recipe in an egg mold, then coat it with an edible white chocolate "eggshell" that they decorate with stars, borders, and rosettes in pretty pastels. The bakers have lots of fun with these cakes, often making each one with different colors and decorations. You'll need an egg-shaped cake pan with a capacity of 8 cups for this cake.*

# easter egg

**MAKES ONE EGG-SHAPED CHEESECAKE (ABOUT 15 X 12 INCHES)**

Four 8-ounce packages
cream cheese (use only full fat),
at room temperature

1²/₃ cups sugar

¼ cup cornstarch

1 tablespoon pure vanilla extract

2 extra-large eggs

¾ cup heavy or whipping cream

12 ounces white chocolate

1 recipe Decorator's Buttercream
(page 28)

Pink, green, and yellow
food coloring (use icing colors
if you have them)

*1.* Preheat the oven to 350°F. Generously butter the bottom and sides of a large 10-cup egg-shaped pan (about 15 x 12 inches). Now, completely line the inside with two pieces of aluminum foil, crisscrossing them and leaving a 3-inch over-hang (this makes it easy to remove the cake after baking). Press the foil gently but firmly into the mold, shaping it into all of its curves so the baked cake will have all of the details of the egg mold. Be careful to not tear the foil—if this happens, start again. Butter the foil, preferably with softened, not melted, butter. (There's no need to wrap the outside of the pan with foil.)

*2.* Put one package of the cream cheese, ⅓ cup of the sugar, and the corn-starch in a large bowl. Beat with an electric mixer on low until creamy, about 3 minutes, scraping the bowl down a few times. Blend in the remaining cream cheese, one package at a time, scraping down the bowl after each one. Increase the mixer speed to medium and beat in the remaining 1⅓ cups sugar, then the vanilla. Add the eggs, one at a time, beating well after adding each one. Beat in the cream just until completely blended. Be careful not to overmix! Spoon the batter into the pan.

*3.* Place in a large shallow pan containing hot water that comes about halfway up the sides of the egg-shaped pan. Bake until the edges are light golden brown and the top is slightly golden tan, about 1¼ hours. Remove the cake from the water bath, transfer to a wire rack, and let cool for 2 hours (just walk away—don't move it). Leave the cake in the pan, cover it loosely with plastic wrap, and refrigerate until it's cold, about 2 hours. Transfer to the freezer until frozen solid, preferably overnight or for at least 4 hours (this makes it safer to remove the cake from the pan and easier to ice it with the white chocolate frosting). If you're not serving the cake the same day, leave it in the freezer.

*4.* To remove the cake from the pan, turn it upside down onto a cake plate or platter without a rim (use one that can go into the freezer). If the cake does not release easily from the pan, place it on a burner over low heat for about 10 seconds, just long enough to melt the butter greasing the pan (use potholders!). Gently peel off the foil and return the unwrapped cake to the freezer for 30 minutes. Melt half of the white chocolate over low heat or in the microwave. Using a narrow metal spatula, spread it over the egg cake in smooth, even strokes. Be sure the spatula is completely dry, as even one drop of water can cause the chocolate to "seize up" and look curdled. Once you have frosted half of the egg with a thin shell, melt the remaining chocolate and finish the other half, making sure to quickly smooth out the places where the halves meet. Refrain from refrosting an area, as white chocolate hardens extra-fast and loses its gloss if reworked too much. Return the cake to the freezer for 1 hour to harden the white chocolate "eggshell" before the final decoration.

*5.* Meanwhile, divide the buttercream into three small bowls. Using only a few drops of food coloring in each bowl, tint the icing in pastel shades: light pink, light yellow, and light green.

*6.* For fancy decorations, fit a pastry bag with a medium closed-star tip (#31) or a medium open-star tip (#32) to make flowers, rosettes, stars, a border of tiny shells around the bottom edge, and zigzag lines in three different pastel colors (page 26). For small decorations, use a small closed-star tip (#24) or a small open-star tip (#17).

*7.* Refrigerate the cake until ready to serve (it takes 2 to 3 hours to defrost in the refrigerator). Slice with a sharp straight-edge knife, not a serrated one. Cover and refrigerate any leftover cake or wrap and freeze for up to 1 month.

## The Junior's Way

Be sure the cake is frozen solid before lifting it out of the mold. Peel off the foil and immediately turn the cake upside down onto a plate that can go into the freezer. Put it back in the freezer while you melt the white chocolate to make its edible "eggshell." Melt only half of the chocolate at a time and frost half the egg first, because white chocolate dries fast. Do not overheat—stop when the chocolate resembles a spreadable buttercream frosting.

Also, when decorating, be aware that the closed-star pastry bag tips make fancier decorations than the open-star ones, with more grooves and details.

*One of the most popular ice cream creations at Junior's soda fountain is a monster version of the banana split called the Banana Royale. Some of those same ingredients of bananas, chocolate, and cream are used to make this impressive cake. The bakers swirl fresh banana purée into the cheesecake batter, flavor it with a little dark rum, then top it all off with chocolate fudge and more bananas. Try it—you'll love it!*

# banana fudge cheesecake

**MAKES ONE 9-INCH CHEESECAKE, ABOUT 2 1/2 INCHES HIGH**

1 recipe 9-inch Junior's Sponge Cake Crust (page 17)

3 large ripe bananas

2 tablespoons fresh lemon juice

Four 8-ounce packages cream cheese (use only full fat), at room temperature

1 2/3 cups sugar

5 tablespoons cornstarch

1 tablespoon pure vanilla extract

1 tablespoon dark rum or 1/2 teaspoon rum extract

2 extra-large eggs

3/4 cup heavy or whipping cream

3 ounces bittersweet or semisweet chocolate, melted (page 23)

2/3 cup fudge ice cream topping

1 teaspoon light corn syrup

*1.* Preheat the oven to 350°F. Generously butter the bottom and sides of a 9-inch springform pan. Wrap the outside with aluminum foil, covering the bottom and extending all the way up the sides. Make and bake the sponge cake crust and leave it in the pan. Keep the oven on.

*2.* Peel, cut into chunks, and purée 2 of the bananas in your food processor (you need 3/4 cup purée). Stir in 1 tablespoon of the lemon juice and set aside.

*3.* Put one package of the cream cheese, 1/3 cup of the sugar, and the cornstarch in a large bowl and beat with an electric mixer on low until creamy, about 3 minutes, scraping down the bowl a couple of times. Blend in the remaining cream cheese, one package at a time, scraping down the bowl after each one. Increase the mixer speed to medium and beat in the remaining 1 1/3 cups sugar, then the vanilla and rum. Add the eggs, one at a time, beating well after adding each one. Beat in the cream only until completely blended. Don't overmix! Measure out 1 cup of batter, stir in the melted chocolate, and set aside. Fold the banana purée into the rest of the batter, then gently spoon over the crust.

**4.** Using a small teaspoon, drop the chocolate batter in small spoonfuls on top of the banana batter, pushing it down slightly as you go. Using a thin, pointed knife, cut through the batter a few times in a "figure 8" design, just until chocolate swirls appear (do not swirl too much or the whole cake will turn light brown and you'll lose the swirls).

**5.** Place in a large shallow pan containing hot water that comes about 1 inch up the sides of the springform. Bake until the edges are light golden brown and the top is slightly golden tan, about 1¼ hours. Remove the cake from the water bath, transfer to a wire rack, and let cool for 2 hours (just walk away—don't move it). Cover with plastic wrap and refrigerate until completely cold, preferably overnight or for at least 4 hours. Freeze the cake (still in the pan) for 1 hour before decorating (the fudge topping will set faster and be easier to handle on the slightly frozen cake).

**6.** To decorate, release and remove the sides of the springform, leaving the cake on the bottom of the pan. Place on a cake plate (use one that can go into the freezer). Combine the ice cream topping and corn syrup in a small saucepan over low heat, stirring just until warm and spreadable (don't overheat or let boil!). Quickly, spread the fudge over the top of the cold cake with a narrow metal spatula, letting a little drip down the sides in a few places, if you like. Return to the freezer until the fudge mirror has set and is no longer sticky (do not cover), about 1 hour.

**7.** Using a straight-edge sharp paring knife and holding the remaining banana slightly on a slant, cut it into 1-inch-thick slices. Toss with the remaining 1 tablespoon lemon juice and arrange in a circle on top of the cake, overlapping the slices as you go. Refrigerate until ready to serve. Slice the cake with a sharp straight-edge knife, not a serrated one. Cover any leftover cake and refrigerate, or remove the banana slices, cover, and freeze.

## The Junior's Way

Look for ripe bananas with bright golden skins, not greenish yellow ones, and without any brown spots (these spots can mean the fruit has been bruised or is overripe and "off" in flavor). Be sure to buy the thick fudge ice cream topping for glazing this cake; chocolate syrup is too thin and doesn't have the deep, dark, rich flavor you want.

*Nothing's more perfect for a Memorial Day or Fourth of July celebration than this patriotic Ol' Glory cheesecake! If you're planning on bringing this to a picnic, forget the whipped cream frosting and assemble the flag directly on the baked cheesecake. Use mini marshmallows for the stars and tote the cake safely in an ice chest.*

# stars & stripes

**MAKES ONE 9-INCH CHEESECAKE, ABOUT 2½ INCHES HIGH**

1 recipe 9-inch Junior's Sponge
Cake Crust (page 17)

**FOR THE CHEESECAKE:**
Four 8-ounce packages
cream cheese (use only full fat),
at room temperature

1²/₃ cups sugar

¼ cup cornstarch

1 tablespoon pure vanilla extract

2 extra-large eggs

¾ cup heavy or whipping cream

**FOR THE WHIPPED CREAM
FROSTING:**
1 tablespoon unflavored
granulated gelatin

2 tablespoons cold water

3 cups cold heavy
or whipping cream

¼ cup sugar

1 tablespoon pure vanilla extract

**FOR THE FLAG DECORATIONS:**
2 half-pints fresh raspberries
(about 6 ounces each)

1 half-pint fresh blueberries
(about 6 ounces)

*1.* Preheat the oven to 350°F. Generously butter the bottom and sides of a 9-inch springform pan. Wrap the outside with aluminum foil, covering the bottom and extending all the way up the sides. Make and bake the sponge cake crust and leave it in the pan. Keep the oven on.

*2.* Put one package of the cream cheese, ⅓ cup of the sugar, and the cornstarch in a large bowl and beat with an electric mixer on low until creamy, about 3 minutes, scraping down the bowl a couple of times. Blend in the remaining cream cheese, one package at a time, stopping to scrape down the bowl after each one. Increase the mixer speed to medium and beat in the remaining 1⅓ cups sugar, then the vanilla. Blend in the eggs, one at a time, beating well after adding each one. Beat in the cream only until completely blended. Be careful not to overmix! Gently spoon the cheese filling over the crust.

*3.* Place in a large shallow pan containing hot water that comes about 1 inch up the sides of the springform. Bake until the edges are light golden brown and the top is slightly golden tan, about 1¼ hours. Remove the cake from the water bath, transfer to a wire rack, and let cool for 2 hours (just walk away—don't move it). Cover with plastic wrap and refrigerate until completely cold, preferably overnight or for at least 4 hours. Transfer to the freezer for at least 2 hours or until ready to decorate the cake (the frosting will set faster and be easier to handle on the slightly frozen cake).

*4.* To decorate, release and remove the sides of the springform, leaving the cake on the bottom of the pan. Place on a cake plate. Make the frosting: Place the gelatin in a heatproof measuring cup, stir in the cold water, and let stand until it swells and thickens. Cook in the microwave on high for about 30 seconds or over a pan of simmering water for about 1 minute, until clear and completely melted. In a medium-size bowl, whip the cream with the mixer on high until it thickens and soft peaks just begin to form. With the mixer still running, add the sugar and beat just until the cream stands up in peaks (don't overmix or the cream will curdle). Beat in the vanilla. Add the melted gelatin all at once and beat until thoroughly incorporated. Transfer about half the frosting to a separate small bowl and refrigerate while you frost the top and sides of the cake with the remaining frosting. Fit a pastry bag with a medium closed-star tip (#31) or medium open-star tip (#32), fill with some of the reserved frosting, and pipe rosettes (page 26) around the edge of the cake bottom, if you wish.

*5.* To make the flag on top, place three straight horizontal rows of raspberries, pointed ends up, about 7 inches long across the bottom half of the cake and three 3½-inch lines in the top right-hand corner. Create a 3-inch blue square with the blueberries as the background for the stars in the upper left-hand corner of the cake. Then pipe whipped-cream stars (as many as 50 if you like) in between and on top of the blueberries, using a small open-star tip (#15).

*6.* Refrigerate until cold and set, at least 2 hours, or until ready to serve. Slice with a sharp straight-edge knife, not a serrated one. Cover any leftover cake and refrigerate. Do not freeze this cake.

*Tiramisu, which means "pick-me-up" in Italian, is a delicious layered creation of ladyfingers, mascarpone, Marsala, strongly brewed espresso, and chocolate. The bakers at Junior's begin with a crust of ladyfingers, then sprinkle it with a syrup that's laced with Kahlúa® instead of Marsala. Next they add a layer of espresso-flavored cheesecake on top. They circle it with more ladyfingers, crown it with a layer of mascarpone, then finish it all off with curls of chocolate and a dusting of cocoa.*

# tiramisu cheesecake

**MAKES ONE 9-INCH CHEESECAKE, ABOUT 3 INCHES HIGH**

*1.* Preheat the oven to 350°F. Generously butter the bottom and sides of a 9-inch springform pan. Wrap the outside of the pan with aluminum foil, covering the bottom and extending all the way up the sides.

*2.* Stir the water and espresso together in a small cup until dissolved. Put one package of the cream cheese, ⅓ cup of the sugar, and the cornstarch in a large bowl. Beat with an electric mixer on low until creamy, about 3 minutes, scraping the bowl down a couple of times. Blend in the remaining cream cheese, one package at a time, scraping down the bowl after each one. Increase the mixer speed to medium and beat in the remaining 1 cup sugar, then the vanilla. Add in the eggs, one at a time, beating well after adding each one. Stir the dissolved coffee into the cream, add to the cream cheese mixture, and beat just until it's completely blended. Be careful not to overmix! Gently spoon the batter into the springform.

*3.* Place in a large shallow pan containing hot water that comes about 1 inch up the sides of the springform. Bake until the edges are light brown and the top is light tan, about 1¼ hours. Remove the cake from the water bath, transfer to a wire rack, and let cool in the pan on a wire rack for 2 hours. Then cover with plastic wrap and refrigerate until completely cold, preferably overnight or for at least 4 hours.

**The Junior's Way**

Here's a tip from Master Baker Michael Goodman for making the ladyfingers stand up straight and tall around the edge of the cake. Spread the cut side of each one with a little mascarpone cream, then stand them up in a ring around the edge. Lightly press each onto the side of the cake; since the cake is cold, the cream sticks fast.

**FOR THE CHEESECAKE:**

1 tablespoon hot water

1 tablespoon instant freeze-dried espresso or coffee

Three 8-ounce packages cream cheese (use only full fat), at room temperature

1 1/3 cups sugar

1/4 cup cornstarch

1 tablespoon pure vanilla extract

2 extra-large eggs

2/3 cup heavy or whipping cream

**FOR THE TIRAMISU SYRUP AND LADYFINGER LAYER:**

1/2 cup hot water

1 tablespoon instant freeze-dried espresso or coffee

2 tablespoons sugar

2 tablespoons Kahlúa or other coffee-flavored liqueur

22 ladyfingers (9 for layering and 13 for the ring around the edge), split

**FOR THE MASCARPONE CREAM:**

1 1/2 teaspoons unflavored granulated gelatin

1 tablespoon cold water

1 1/2 cups cold heavy or whipping cream

2 tablespoons sugar

1 tablespoon pure vanilla extract

One 8- to 10-ounce carton mascarpone cheese

**FOR THE TOPPING:**

4 ounces bittersweet or semisweet chocolate made into Chocolate Curls (page 21)

1 tablespoon unsweetened cocoa powder

*4.* Make the tiramisu syrup. Combine the water and espresso in a small sauce-pan until dissolved. Add the sugar and Kahlúa, bring to a boil over medium-high heat, reduce the heat to medium, and let simmer, uncovered, for 3 minutes, stirring a few times. Top the cold cheesecake (still in the pan) with a layer of split ladyfingers, rounded-side down (you will need 18 halves). Drizzle evenly with all of the syrup. Transfer the cake to the freezer until completely frozen, at least overnight and/or until ready to assemble.

*5.* When you're ready to assemble the cake, make the mascarpone cream. Place the gelatin in a heatproof measuring cup, stir in the cold water, and let stand until it swells and thickens. Cook in the microwave on high for about 30 seconds or over a pan of simmering water for about 1 minute, until clear and completely melted. In a medium-size bowl, whip the cream with the mixer on high until it thickens and soft peaks just begin to form. With the mixer still running, add the sugar and beat just until the cream stands up in peaks (don't overmix or the cream will curdle). Beat in the vanilla. Add the melted gelatin all at once and beat until thoroughly incorporated. Gently fold in the mascarpone with a rubber spatula.

*6.* Remove the cake from the freezer and let it stand at room temperature about 10 minutes. Release and remove the sides of the springform, then remove the cheesecake from the bottom of the pan (see Solutions on page 15). Transfer to a cake plate. To attach the remaining ladyfingers (26 halves) to the outside of the cake, spread a thin layer of the mascarpone cream over the flat split sides of the ladyfingers. Stand them up around the edge of the cake, rounded-side out, pressing each one gently in place. Spoon the remaining mascarpone on top of the cake and gently even out with a metal spatula; it will come up almost to the top of the ladyfingers. Since the cheesecake is still very cold, the mascarpone cream will set fast.

*7.* To decorate, cover the top of the cake with the chocolate curls, then sprinkle evenly with the cocoa. Refrigerate for at least 2 hours, until the mascarpone layer is cold and set and the cheesecake layer has defrosted enough to slice eas-ily. Slice with a sharp straight-edge knife, not a serrated one. Cover any leftover cake and refrigerate or wrap and freeze for up to 1 month.

*This is a perfect choice for Thanksgiving, swirled as it is with cranberry sauce and topped with dried cranberries and white chocolate chips.*

# white chocolate & cranberry holiday cake

**MAKES ONE 9-INCH CHEESECAKE, ABOUT 2½ INCHES HIGH**

1 recipe 9-inch Junior's Sponge Cake Crust (page 17)

1 cup canned jellied cranberry sauce

3 tablespoons plus 1 teaspoon cornstarch

Three 8-ounce packages cream cheese (use only full fat), at room temperature

1⅓ cups sugar

1 tablespoon pure vanilla extract

2 extra-large eggs

8 ounces white chocolate, melted (page 23) and slightly cooled

⅔ cup heavy or whipping cream

**FOR THE TOPPING:**

¾ cup dried cranberries

Boiling water

1 cup white chocolate chips

*1.* Preheat the oven to 350°F. Generously butter the bottom and sides of a 9-inch springform pan. Wrap the outside with aluminum foil, covering the bottom and extending all the way up the sides. Make and bake the sponge cake crust and leave it in the pan. Keep the oven on.

*2.* Break up the cranberry sauce with a spoon, add the 1 teaspoon of cornstarch, and stir until almost smooth.

*3.* Put one package of the cream cheese, ⅓ cup of the sugar, and the remaining 3 tablespoons cornstarch in a large bowl. Beat with an electric mixer on low until creamy, about 3 minutes, scraping down the bowl a few times. Beat in the remaining cream cheese, one package at a time, scraping down the bowl after adding each one. Increase the mixer speed to medium and beat in the remaining 1 cup sugar, then the vanilla. Add the eggs, one at a time, beating well after adding each one. Blend in the melted white chocolate, then the cream just until completely blended. Don't overmix! Gently spoon the cheese filling evenly over the crust.

*4.* Using a small spoon, drop the cranberry sauce in spoonfuls on top of the batter, pushing it down slightly as you go. Using a thin, pointed knife, cut through the batter a few times, just until red swirls appear (don't swirl too much or the whole cake will turn pink and you'll lose the swirls).

*5.* Place in a large shallow pan containing hot water that comes about 1 inch up the sides of the springform. Bake until the edges are light golden brown and the top is slightly golden tan with cranberry swirls, about 1¼ hours. Remove

*Celebration Cheesecakes* **95**

the cake from the water bath, transfer to a wire rack, and let cool for 2 hours (just walk away—don't move it). Refrigerate until completely cold, preferably overnight or for at least 4 hours.

*6.* Meanwhile, put the dried cranberries in a small bowl, cover with boiling water, and let soak until plump, about 30 minutes. Strain, shake off any excess water, and spread out on paper towels to dry.

*7.* To decorate the cake, release and remove the sides of the pan, leaving the cake on the bottom. Make a 2-inch border of white chocolate chips and cranberries around the top edge of the cake and scatter a few more cranberries near the center of the cake. Return the cake to the refrigerator until serving time. Slice with a sharp straight-edge knife, not a serrated one. Cover any leftover cake and refrigerate, or wrap and freeze for up to 1 month.

*The Junior's Way*

Be sure to buy the smooth jellied cranberry sauce for this cake, not the whole berry kind. Then take a spoon (not a whisk, which might break the gel) and stir gently until it's broken into small pieces and relatively smooth.

_If pumpkin pie is one of your favorites, you'll love this cake! In fact, it's more of a pie than a cake. The shortbread crust is reminiscent of a buttery piecrust. It's topped with a creamy pumpkin mousse that makes it even more special._

# pumpkin mousse cheesecake

1 recipe 9-inch Junior's
Shortbread Crust (page 18)

FOR THE CHEESECAKE:

¾ cup canned pumpkin purée
(not canned pumpkin pie mix)

1 teaspoon pumpkin pie spice

Three 8-ounce packages
cream cheese (use only full fat),
at room temperature

1⅓ cups sugar

3 tablespoons cornstarch

1 tablespoon pure vanilla extract

2 extra-large eggs

⅔ cup heavy or whipping cream

FOR THE PUMPKIN MOUSSE
AND TOPPING:

½ cup canned pumpkin purée
(not canned pumpkin pie mix)

¼ teaspoon pumpkin pie spice

2 teaspoons unflavored
granulated gelatin

2 tablespoons cold water

2 cups heavy or whipping cream

¼ cup sugar

1 tablespoon pure vanilla extract

4 large cinnamon graham crackers,
crushed (½ cup crumbs)

1 cup coarsely chopped walnuts

MAKES ONE 9-INCH CHEESECAKE, ABOUT 2½ INCHES HIGH

_1._ Preheat the oven to 350°F. Generously butter the bottom and sides of a 9-inch springform pan. Wrap the outside with aluminum foil, covering the bottom and extending all the way up the sides. Make and bake the shortbread crust and leave in the pan. Keep the oven on.

_2._ Make the cheesecake. Mix the pumpkin purée and pumpkin pie spice together in a small bowl and let stand. Put one package of the cream cheese, ⅓ cup of the sugar, and the cornstarch in a large bowl. Beat with an electric mixer on low until creamy, about 3 minutes, scraping the bowl down a few times. Blend in the remaining cream cheese, one package at a time, scraping down the bowl after each one. Increase the mixer speed to medium and beat in the remaining 1 cup sugar, then the vanilla. Add the eggs, one at a time, beating well after adding each one. Beat in the cream just until completely blended. Be careful not to overmix!

_3._ Remove 1 cup of this white batter and set aside. On low speed, blend the spiced pumpkin purée into the remaining batter. Gently spoon this on top of the crust. Using a teaspoon, drop the white batter in small spoonfuls on top of the pumpkin batter, pushing it down slightly as you go. Using a thin, pointed knife, cut through the batter a few times in a "figure 8" design, just until white swirls appear.

_4._ Place in a large shallow pan containing hot water that comes about 1 inch up the sides of the springform. Bake until the edges are light golden brown and the top is tan with light golden swirls, about 1¼ hours. Remove the cake from the water bath, transfer to a wire rack, and let cool for 2 hours (just walk away—don't move it). Leave the cake in the pan, cover it loosely with plastic wrap, and refrigerate until completely cold, about 4 hours.

*5.* Meanwhile, make the pumpkin mousse. Mix the pumpkin with the pumpkin pie spice in a small bowl and set aside. Place the gelatin in a heatproof measuring cup, stir in the cold water, and let stand until it thickens. Cook in the microwave on high for about 30 seconds or place over a pan of simmering water for about 1 minute, until completely melted. Set aside to cool. In a large clean bowl with clean beaters, whip the cream with the mixer on high just until it thickens and peaks begin to form. With the mixer still running, add the sugar and vanilla. Blend in the pumpkin purée and beat until fluffy with slightly firm peaks. Beat in the dissolved gelatin all at once, just until it disappears. Watch carefully and do not overbeat at this stage. It's now ready to spoon onto the chilled cake; if the cake is not yet cold, refrigerate the mousse (it's best if used within 1 hour).

*6.* Remove the cake from the refrigerator, leaving it in the pan. Spoon the pumpkin mousse on top of the cake (it will come up to the top of the pan). Spread it out to the sides with a metal spatula. Cover the top evenly with the graham cracker crumbs and decorate with a circle of chopped walnuts. Cover with plastic wrap and freeze the cake until the mousse is firm and set, preferably overnight or at least 4 hours. If you're not serving the cake the same day, leave it in the freezer.

*7.* About 2 hours before serving, let the cake stand at room temperature for about 15 minutes, just long enough to release the sides of the springform. Transfer to a cake plate, leaving the cake on the bottom of the pan. Refrigerate (do not cover) until time to serve (it'll take about 2 hours to thaw in the refrigerator so you can slice it easily). Refrigerate any leftover cake or wrap and return to the freezer for up to a month.

*This cheesecake is all dressed up for the holidays. It's easy to make, fast to decorate, and looks like a masterpiece! We've whirled strawberry purée throughout and baked it in a tree shape to make it even more festive. Laden it with garlands of red and green holiday candies and hang peppermint ornaments on its branches. Then have yourself a very merry Christmas! You'll need a tree-shaped cake pan with a capacity of 8 cups to make this.*

# christmas tree

MAKES ONE TREE-SHAPED CHEESECAKE (ABOUT 15 X 12 INCHES)

8 ounces dry-pack frozen whole strawberries (unsweetened, not in syrup), thawed and drained well (about 1 cup)

¼ cup plus 1 teaspoon cornstarch

Three 8-ounce packages cream cheese (use only full fat), at room temperature

1⅓ cups sugar

1 tablespoon pure vanilla extract

2 extra-large eggs

¾ cup heavy or whipping cream

1 cup small red and green coated chocolate candies, such as M&M's®

Assorted holiday round candies for ornaments, about 1-inch in diameter (such as round peppermint swirls)

*1.* Preheat the oven to 350°F. Generously butter the bottom and sides of an 8-cup tree-shaped pan. Completely line the inside of the pan with aluminum foil, using two pieces and crisscrossing them. Press the foil gently into all of its branches and curves so the baked cake will have all of the details of the mold. Don't tear the foil; if you do, start over with new foil. Coat the foil well with softened butter. Leave a 3-inch overhang of foil (this makes it easy to remove the cake after baking and freezing). There's no need to wrap the outside of the pan.

*2.* Pulse the thawed strawberries in a food processor until smooth (you need ¾ cup of purée). Stir in 1 teaspoon of the cornstarch and set aside. It will thicken slightly as it stands.

*3.* Put one package of the cream cheese, ⅓ cup of the sugar, and the remaining ¼ cup cornstarch in a large bowl. Beat with an electric mixer on low until creamy, about 3 minutes, scraping the bowl down a few times. Blend in the remaining cream cheese, one package at a time, scraping down the bowl after each one. Increase the mixer speed to medium and beat in the remaining 1 cup sugar, then the vanilla. Add the eggs, one at a time, beating well after adding each one. Beat in the cream just until completely blended. Be careful not to overmix!

*4.* Spread half the cheese filling in tree pan. Using a teaspoon, drop the strawberry purée in small spoonfuls on top of the batter, pushing it down slightly as

you go. Using a thin, pointed knife, cut through the batter a few times in a "figure 8" design, just until red swirls appear (don't mix in the purée completely or the whole cake will turn pink and you'll lose the swirls). Gently and carefully, spread the remaining cheese filling on top.

5. Place in a large shallow pan containing hot water that comes about halfway up the sides of the tree pan. Bake until the edges are light golden brown and the top is slightly golden tan, about 1 hour. Remove the cake from the water bath, transfer to a wire rack, and let cool for 2 hours (just walk away—don't move it). Leave the cake in the pan, cover it loosely with plastic wrap, and refrigerate until it's cold, at least 4 hours. Transfer to the freezer until frozen solid, preferably overnight or at least 4 hours. If you're not serving the cake the same day, leave it in the freezer.

6. To remove the cake from the pan, turn it upside down onto a cake plate or a platter without a rim. If the cake does not release easily from the pan, place it on a burner over low heat for about 10 seconds, just long enough to melt the butter greasing the pan (use potholders!). Gently peel away the foil.

7. To decorate, make the garlands with small red candies and fill in the trunk of the tree with some small green candies. Hang larger round candy ornaments on its branches. Refrigerate until ready to serve (it will take about 2 hours to thaw in the refrigerator). Slice with a sharp straight-edge knife, not a serrated one. Cover and refrigerate any leftover cake or wrap and freeze for up to 1 month.

## The Junior's Way

To decorate the tree, use red and green coated chocolate candies for the trunk of the tree and the garlands. Have fun hanging other decorative candy ornaments on its branches.

*The authentic version of Black Forest Cake, known as schwarzwalder Kirschtorte in German, is a towering creation of several layers of chocolate cake, usually sprinkled with plenty of the cherry brandy called kirsch, and filled with whipped cream and potent Bing cherries that have been left to soak in kirsch for several days. Junior's creation adds lots of Bing cherries and a splash of kirsch to the cheesecake batter. They finish it off with a chocolate fudge mirror and a web of dark chocolate.*

# black forest cheesecake

**MAKES ONE 9-INCH CHEESECAKE, ABOUT 2 1/2 INCHES HIGH**

1 recipe 9-inch Dark Chocolate Sponge Cake Crust (page 17)

**FOR THE CHERRY FILLING:**
3/4 cup purple grape juice
2 tablespoons cornstarch
1 tablespoon sugar
2 teaspoons fresh lemon juice
16 ounces (about 1 1/2 cups) frozen pitted Bing cherries (unsweetened, not in syrup), thawed and drained well

**FOR THE CHEESECAKE:**
Three 8-ounce packages cream cheese (use only full fat), at room temperature
1 1/3 cups sugar
1/4 cup cornstarch
1 tablespoon pure vanilla extract
1 teaspoon cherry brandy (kirsch)
2 extra-large eggs
2/3 cup heavy or whipping cream

*1.* Preheat the oven to 350°F. Generously butter the bottom and sides of a 9-inch springform pan. Wrap the outside with aluminum foil, covering the bottom and extending all the way up the sides. Make and bake the sponge cake crust and leave it in the pan. Keep the oven on.

*2.* Make the cherry filling. Stir the grape juice and cornstarch together in a small saucepan until completely dissolved, then stir in the sugar. Bring to a full boil over medium heat. Cook and stir constantly until the mixture turns clear and thickens, about 2 minutes (very important!). Remove from the heat and stir in the lemon juice, then gently fold in the cherries. Set aside to cool while you make the cake.

*3.* Put one package of the cream cheese, 1/3 cup of the sugar, and the cornstarch in a large bowl. Beat with an electric mixer on low until creamy, about 3 minutes, scraping it down a few times. Beat in the remaining cream cheese one package at a time, scraping down the bowl after each. Increase the mixer speed to medium and beat in the remaining 1 cup sugar, then the vanilla and brandy. Add the eggs, one at a time, beating well after adding each one. Beat in the cream just until completely blended. Be careful not to overmix! Gently fold the cherry filling into the cheesecake batter, then spread it over the crust.

*4.* Place in a large shallow pan containing hot water that comes about 1 inch up the sides of the springform. Bake until the edges are light golden brown and the top is slightly golden tan, about 1¼ hours. Remove the cake from the water bath, transfer to a wire rack, and let cool for 2 hours (just walk away—don't move it). Cover the cake loosely with plastic wrap and refrigerate until completely cold, preferably overnight or at least 4 hours. Transfer to the freezer for 1 hour before decorating (the fudge mirror sets faster and is easier to handle on the slightly frozen cake).

*5.* Make the topping. Combine the ice cream topping and corn syrup in a small saucepan over low heat, stirring just until warm and spreadable (don't overheat or let boil!). With the cake still in the pan, quickly spread the fudge over the top of the cold cake with a narrow metal spatula. Now top with a chocolate web following the directions on page 22, making the lines about ½ inch apart. Return the cake to the freezer until the mirror and web have set, about 1 hour (do not cover).

FOR THE TOPPING:

½ cup fudge ice cream topping (not chocolate syrup)

1 teaspoon light corn syrup

4 ounces bittersweet or semisweet chocolate, melted (page 23)

10 to 12 fresh Bing cherries with stems or frozen cherries, thawed and drained well

*6.* To serve, release and remove the sides of the springform, leaving the cake on the bottom of the pan. Place on a serving plate. Refrigerate until ready to serve. Decorate the center with a mound of fresh cherries right before serving. Slice with a sharp straight-edge knife, not a serrated one. Refrigerate any leftover cake or wrap and freeze for up to 1 month.

*The Junior's Way*

"Don't worry if the center of the cake is a little soft when you cut it," advises Alan Rosen. "This tender center makes the cake even more delicious when you eat it!"

# We Love Chocolate!

Like most folks, everyone at Junior's loves chocolate! So it's no surprise that almost every time that I'm in the bakery, there seem to be hundreds of chocolate cheesecakes coming out of the ovens. Is plain chocolate your favorite? Then enjoy it in all its delicious simplicity or showered with chocolate curls and drizzled with a chocolate web on top. Or try a slice of Brownie Swirl, with small bites of rich brownies throughout. If you love chocolate candy, you won't be able to resist baking up Junior's Candy Bar Explosion cake. And if you enjoy splurging on a rocky road sundae, try the cheesecake rendition.

*If you like chocolate, you'll love this one! The bakers flavor both the sponge cake crust and cream cheese filling with chocolate, then they top it all off with even more chocolate, this time with a fudge mirror and a fancy crosshatch web on top. Decadent? You bet, the oh-so-yummy Junior's way.*

# triple chocolate cheesecake

**MAKES ONE 9-INCH CHEESECAKE, ABOUT 2 1/2 INCHES HIGH**

1 recipe 9-inch Dark Chocolate Sponge Cake Crust (page 17)

**FOR THE CHEESECAKE:**

10 ounces bittersweet or semisweet chocolate

Four 8-ounce packages cream cheese (use only full fat), at room temperature

1 2/3 cups sugar

1/3 cup cornstarch

1 tablespoon pure vanilla extract

2 extra-large eggs

3/4 cup heavy or whipping cream

**FOR THE FUDGE MIRROR:**

1/2 cup fudge ice cream topping (not chocolate syrup)

1 teaspoon light corn syrup

**FOR THE CHOCOLATE WEB:**

4 ounces bittersweet or semisweet chocolate

*1.* Preheat the oven to 350°F. Generously butter the bottom and sides of a 9-inch springform pan. Wrap the outside with aluminum foil, covering the bottom and extending all the way up the sides. Make and bake the cake crust and leave it in the pan. Keep the oven on.

*2.* Melt the chocolate (page 23) and set aside to cool. Put one package of the cream cheese, 1/3 cup of the sugar, and the cornstarch in a large bowl. Beat with an electric mixer on low until creamy, about 3 minutes, scraping down the bowl several times. Blend in the remaining cream cheese, one package at a time, scraping down the bowl after each one. Increase the mixer speed to medium and beat in the remaining 1 1/3 cups sugar, then the vanilla. Blend in the eggs, one at a time, beating well after adding each one. Beat in the melted chocolate, then the cream, just until completely blended. Don't overmix! Gently spoon the batter on top of the crust.

*3.* Place the cake in a large shallow pan containing hot water that comes about 1 inch up the sides of the springform. Bake until the edges look baked and the top of the cake appears set, about 1 1/4 hours. Remove the cake from the water bath, transfer to a wire rack, and let cool for 2 hours (just walk away—don't move it). Leave the cake in the pan, cover loosely with plastic wrap, and refrigerate until completely cold, preferably overnight or at least 4 hours. Transfer to the freezer for 1 hour.

*4.* Make the fudge mirror. Stir the fudge topping and corn syrup in a small saucepan over low heat just until warm and spreadable (don't let it boil). Evenly spread over the top of the cake, then return to the freezer (do not cover) until the mirror has set and is no longer sticky, about 1 hour.

*5.* Release and remove the sides of the springform, leaving the cake on the bottom of the pan. Place on a cake plate. Decorate with a chocolate web. Heat the chocolate just until it melts (page 23). Following the directions on page 22, pipe a web of melted chocolate on top of the mirror, making the lines about ⅜ inch apart.

*6.* Refrigerate the cake until ready to serve. Slice with a sharp straight-edge knife, not a serrated one. Cover any leftover cake and refrigerate or freeze up to 1 month.

*The Junior's Way*

When making the chocolate web from melted chocolate, be creative. Instead of using only dark chocolate for all of the crosshatching, you could pipe the vertical stripes of dark chocolate, then use either white chocolate or milk chocolate to make contrasting horizontal crosshatch lines.

*One of the first (if not the first) brownie recipe appeared in 1906 in The Boston Cooking-School Book. There have been countless versions ever since—some almost cakelike, others dark, rich, and fudgy. As you might expect, Junior's makes their brownies with lots of dark bittersweet chocolate, plus plenty of butter, sugar, and eggs. Here, they take their brownies and turn them into a crust for the cheesecake, then scatter mini-bites of brownies throughout the filling. Needless to say, this one's over-the-top delicious!*

# brownie swirl

**MAKES ONE 9-INCH CHEESECAKE, ABOUT 3 INCHES HIGH**

**FOR THE BROWNIE CRUST
AND BROWNIE BITES:**

8 ounces bittersweet
or semisweet chocolate

1 cup (2 sticks) unsalted butter

1½ cups all-purpose flour

1 teaspoon salt

6 extra-large eggs

2 cups sugar

1 tablespoon pure vanilla extract

**FOR THE CHEESECAKE:**

Three 8-ounce packages
cream cheese (use only full fat),
at room temperature

1⅓ cups sugar

3 tablespoons cornstarch

1 tablespoon pure vanilla extract

2 extra-large eggs

⅔ cup heavy or whipping cream,
plus 1 tablespoon for brushing

2 ounces bittersweet
or semisweet chocolate

1 cup coarsely chopped walnuts

*1.* Preheat the oven to 350°F. Generously butter the bottom and sides of a 9-inch springform pan and an 8-inch square baking pan. Line the baking pan (but not the springform) with parchment or waxed paper, leaving a 1-inch overhang over the sides. Wrap the outside of the springform with aluminum foil, covering the bottom and extending all the way up the sides.

*2.* To make the brownies, melt the chocolate (page 23) with the butter and let cool. In a small bowl, combine the flour and salt. In a large bowl, beat the eggs with an electric mixer on high until light yellow and thick, about 3 minutes. With the mixer still running, gradually add the sugar, then the chocolate mixture and vanilla. Reduce the speed to low and blend in the flour mixture just until it disappears.

*3.* Spread 2 cups of the batter in the springform to make the crust and the rest in the baking pan. Bake just until set around the sides, about 10 minutes for the crust and 25 minutes for the baking pan. (The centers will be slightly soft.) Let cool on a wire rack for 1 hour. Leave the brownie crust in the springform. Lift the brownies out of the square pan onto a plate, using the paper hanging over the sides as handles. Cover both the crust and the square of brownies with plastic wrap and refrigerate overnight.

*4.* Cut the square of brownies with a serrated knife into 1-inch squares and set aside. Put one package of the cream cheese, ⅓ cup of the sugar, and the cornstarch in a large bowl. Beat with an electric mixer on low until creamy, about 3 minutes, scraping down the bowl several times. Blend in the remaining cream cheese, one package at a time, scraping down the bowl after each one. Increase the mixer speed to medium and beat in the remaining 1 cup sugar, then the vanilla. Blend in the eggs, one at a time, beating well after adding each one. Beat in the ⅔ cup of cream just until completely blended. Don't overmix! Transfer 1 cup of the batter to a small bowl and set aside for the chocolate swirls.

*5.* Cover the chocolate brownie crust in the pan with small brownie bites (12 to 16), covering as much of the crust as possible. Use only one layer of brownie bites in order to leave plenty of room for the cheesecake batter. (Eat the rest of the brownies!) Gently spoon the white batter over the brownie bites.

*6.* Now make the chocolate swirls. Melt the chocolate (page 23) and stir into the reserved white batter until completely blended. Using a teaspoon, drop the chocolate batter on top of the white batter, pushing it down slightly as you go. Using a thin, pointed knife, cut through the batter a few times in a swirling "figure 8" design, just until chocolate swirls appear.

*7.* Place the cake in a large shallow pan containing hot water that comes about 1 inch up the sides of the springform. Bake until the edges are light golden brown and the top of the cake has golden and dark chocolate swirls, about 1¼ hours. Remove the cake from the water bath, transfer to a wire rack, and let cool for 2 hours (just walk away—don't move it). Leave the cake in the pan, cover loosely with plastic wrap, and refrigerate until completely cold, at least 4 hours or preferably overnight.

*8.* To serve, release and remove the sides of the springform, leaving the cake on the bottom of the pan. Place on a cake plate. Brush the remaining 1 tablespoon cream in a 1-inch border around the top edge of the cake (this helps keep the nuts in place). Sprinkle the walnuts over the cream, pressing the nuts down gently, making a 1-inch border around the top outside edge. Refrigerate until ready to serve. Slice with a sharp straight-edge knife, not a serrated one. Cover leftover cake and refrigerate or freeze up to 1 month.

*Remember those old-fashioned glass marbles? They have swirls of light and dark colors, similar to the ones in this marble cake. You guessed it—that's how this cake got its name. The first marble cakes from the late 1800s were made with two batters. One was vanilla, just like in today's cakes. But the second darker batter was often flavored with molasses, spices, or even raisins. In Junior's marble cheesecakes, those dark swirls are always deep, rich chocolate. "When you want to make a very big impression, bake this cheesecake!" suggests Alan Rosen.*

# chocolate marble cheesecake

**MAKES ONE 9-INCH CHEESECAKE, ABOUT 2½ INCHES HIGH**

1 recipe 9-inch Dark Chocolate Sponge Cake Crust (page 17)

Four 8-ounce packages cream cheese (use only full fat), at room temperature

1²/₃ cups sugar

¹/₃ cup cornstarch

1 tablespoon pure vanilla extract

2 extra-large eggs

³/₄ cup heavy or whipping cream

6 ounces bittersweet or semisweet chocolate

1 recipe Chocolate Curls (page 21)

*1.* Preheat the oven to 350°F. Generously butter the bottom and sides of a 9-inch springform pan. Wrap the outside of the pan with aluminum foil, covering the bottom and extending all the way up the sides. Make and bake the cake crust and leave it in the pan. Keep the oven on.

*2.* Put one package of the cream cheese, ¹/₃ cup of the sugar, and the cornstarch in a large bowl. Beat with an electric mixer on low until creamy, about 3 minutes, scraping down the bowl several times. Blend in the remaining cream cheese, one package at a time, scraping down the bowl after each one. Increase the mixer speed to medium and beat in the remaining 1¹/₃ cups sugar, then the vanilla. Blend in the eggs, one at a time, beating well after adding each one, then add the cream, beating just until completely blended. Don't overmix!

*3.* Melt the chocolate (page 23). Transfer half the white batter (about 4 cups) to a second bowl and gently stir in the melted chocolate. Keep stirring until all the white batter is "colored" chocolate.

*4.* Gently spoon a third of both batters on top of the crust, alternating table-spoonfuls of chocolate and vanilla. Continue with the second layer, placing alternating colors of batter on top of the first layer. Repeat, making a third layer and using up all of both batters. Now, take a thin, pointed knife and cut through the batter in a swirling "figure 8" design, turning the knife as you go. Stop when the swirls resemble designs in those old-fashioned marbles. Don't swirl the batters together too much or you'll get a light chocolate cake instead of a marbled one.

*5.* Place the cake in a large shallow pan containing hot water that comes about 1 inch up the sides of the springform. Bake until the edges are light golden brown and the top of the cake has golden and dark chocolate swirls, about 1¼ hours. Remove the cake from the water bath, transfer to a wire rack, and let cool for 2 hours (just walk away—don't move it). Leave the cake in the pan, cover loosely with plastic wrap, and refrigerate until completely cold, preferably overnight or at least 4 hours.

*6.* To decorate, release and remove the sides of the springform, leaving the cake on the bottom of the pan. Place on a cake plate. Make the chocolate curls and place a 1½-inch ring of them around the outside rim of the cake. Be sure to keep plenty of the marbled swirls showing in the center. Refrigerate until ready to serve. Slice with a sharp straight-edge knife, not a serrated one. Cover any leftover cake and refrigerate or freeze for up to 1 month.

*The Junior's Way*

Use the smallest, most pointed knife you have to swirl the white and chocolate batters together. As you make "figure-8's" through the batter, hold the knife at an angle and swirl as you go.

*Junior's has been making this cake for a long time. The idea is simple: take their famous cheesecake but skip the sponge cake layer—you don't need it for this one. Whip up a chocolate mousse from heavy cream and the best bittersweet or semisweet chocolate you can find. Then spoon a traditional chocolate ganache over all and decorate with mini chips. Junior's covers the sides with the chips, but I've found it's easier to put them on top.*

# chocolate mousse cheesecake

## FOR THE CHEESECAKE:

Three 8-ounce packages
cream cheese (use only full fat),
at room temperature

1 1/3 cups sugar

3 tablespoons cornstarch

1 tablespoon pure vanilla extract

2 extra-large eggs

2/3 cup heavy or whipping cream

## FOR THE CHOCOLATE MOUSSE:

1 tablespoon unflavored
granulated gelatin

2 tablespoons cold water

8 ounces bittersweet
or semisweet chocolate

3 cups heavy or whipping cream

3 tablespoons sugar

1 tablespoon pure vanilla extract

## FOR THE TOPPING:

1 recipe Traditional
Chocolate Ganache (page 24)

1 cup mini chocolate chips

1/2 cup Marshmallow Fluff®
(optional)

**MAKES ONE 9-INCH CHEESECAKE, ABOUT 3 INCHES HIGH**

*1.* Preheat the oven to 350°F. Generously butter the bottom and sides of a 9-inch springform pan. Wrap the outside with aluminum foil, covering the bottom and extending all the way up the sides.

*2.* Put one package of the cream cheese, 1/3 cup of the sugar, and the cornstarch in a large bowl. Beat with an electric mixer on low until creamy, about 3 minutes, scraping down the bowl several times. Blend in the remaining cream cheese, one package at a time, scraping down the bowl after each one. Increase the mixer speed to medium and beat in the remaining 1 cup sugar, then the vanilla. Blend in the eggs, one at a time, beating well after adding each one. Beat in the cream just until completely blended. Be careful not to overmix! Gently spoon the batter into the prepared pan.

*3.* Place the cake in a large shallow pan containing hot water that comes about 1 inch up the sides of the springform. Bake until the edges are light golden brown and the top of the cake is slightly golden tan, about 1¼ hours. Remove the cake from the water bath, transfer to a wire rack, and let cool for 2 hours (just walk away—don't move it). Leave the cake in the pan, cover loosely with plastic wrap, and refrigerate until cold and set, about 4 hours.

*This is exactly what the name promises: Junior's #1 champion cheesecake with plenty of extra chocolate and crunch. For the chocolate part, bake the cake in a chocolate sponge crust, then smear the top of the cake with hot fudge. Sprinkle crumbled Heath bars on top and finish it all off with a web of bittersweet chocolate. Go ahead: cut a slice and get ready for an over-the-top delicious experience!*

# chocolate crunch cheesecake

**MAKES ONE 9-INCH CHEESECAKE, ABOUT 2 1/2 INCHES HIGH**

1 recipe 9-inch Dark Chocolate Sponge Cake Crust (page 17)

Four 8-ounce packages cream cheese (use only full fat), at room temperature

1 2/3 cups sugar

1/4 cup cornstarch

1 tablespoon pure vanilla extract

2 extra-large eggs

3/4 cup heavy or whipping cream

Three 1.4-ounce Heath milk chocolate English toffee candy bars

1/2 cup hot fudge ice cream topping (not chocolate syrup)

**FOR THE CHOCOLATE WEB:**

4 ounces bittersweet or semisweet chocolate, melted (page 23)

*1.* Preheat the oven to 350°F. Generously butter the bottom and sides of a 9-inch springform pan. Wrap the outside of the pan with aluminum foil, covering the bottom and extending all the way up the sides. Make and bake the cake crust and leave it in the pan. Keep the oven on.

*2.* Put one package of the cream cheese, 1/3 cup of the sugar, and the cornstarch in a large bowl. Beat with an electric mixer on low until creamy, about 3 minutes, scraping down the bowl several times. Blend in the remaining cream cheese, one package at a time, scraping down the bowl after each one. Increase the mixer speed to medium and beat in the remaining 1 1/3 cups sugar, then the vanilla. Blend in the eggs, one at a time, beating well after adding each one. Beat in the cream just until completely blended. Don't overmix! Gently spoon the batter over the chocolate crust.

*3.* Place the cake in a large shallow pan containing hot water that comes about 1 inch up the sides of the springform. Bake until the edges are light golden brown and the top of the cake is slightly golden tan, about 1 1/4 hours. Remove the cake from the water bath, transfer to a wire rack, and let cool for 2 hours (just walk away—don't move it). Leave the cake in the pan, cover loosely with plastic wrap, and refrigerate, preferably overnight or at least 4 hours, until cold and firm. Transfer the cake to the freezer for 1 hour.

*4.* While the cake is in the freezer, chop the Heath bars coarsely (small enough so you can pipe a chocolate web on top of them—but not so much that they turn into fine crumbs).

*5.* Remove the sides of the springform. Leave the cake on the bottom of the pan and place on a cake plate (use one that can go into the freezer). In a small saucepan over low heat, warm the fudge ice cream topping just until spoonable (do not overheat!). Spread the fudge topping over the top of the cake. Be sure to work fast while the cake is still icy cold so the fudge sets quickly. Sprinkle the candy crumbs evenly over the top.

*6.* To make the web, use a #1 or #2 frosting tip in a pastry bag, or make a paper cone of waxed paper and snip off the tip, leaving a hole about ⅛ inch wide in the bottom. Fill with the warm melted chocolate and pipe quickly, making thin lines, ⅜ inch apart, in a crosshatch web pattern. For the finishing touch, pipe several narrow chocolate drips all around the side of the cake (they should look as if they're dripping off of the top—pipe some short ones and some longer ones). Return the cake to the freezer for 1 hour to set the decorations, then refrigerate until ready to serve. Slice with a sharp straight-edge knife, not a serrated one. Cover any leftover cake and refrigerate or freeze up to 1 month.

*The Junior's Way*

**Don't worry if the lines of your chocolate web aren't perfectly straight—the cake looks more homemade that way.**

*The idea of this cheesecake just might have come from the soda fountain at Junior's. Their chocolate mile-high sundaes frequently begin with chocolate ice cream and they use lots of ice cream toppings and nuts. Whatever the origin of this cheesecake, it's another Junior's masterpiece!*

# chocolate, caramel & walnut cheesecake

**MAKES ONE 9-INCH CHEESECAKE, ABOUT 2 1/2 INCHES HIGH**

1 recipe 9-inch Dark Chocolate Sponge Cake Crust (page 17)

10 ounces bittersweet or semisweet chocolate

Four 8-ounce packages cream cheese (use only full fat), at room temperature

1 2/3 cups sugar

1/3 cup cornstarch

1 tablespoon pure vanilla extract

2 extra-large eggs

3/4 cup heavy or whipping cream

1 cup walnut halves

2/3 cup caramel ice cream topping

1 teaspoon light corn syrup

*1.* Preheat the oven to 350°F. Generously butter the bottom and sides of a 9-inch springform pan. Wrap the outside with aluminum foil, covering the bottom and extending all the way up the sides. Make and bake the cake crust and leave it in the pan. Keep the oven on.

*2.* Melt the chocolate (page 23) and set aside to cool. Put one package of the cream cheese, 1/3 cup of the sugar, and the cornstarch in a large bowl. Beat with an electric mixer on low until creamy, about 3 minutes, scraping down the bowl several times. Blend in the remaining cream cheese, one package at a time, scraping down the bowl after each one. Increase the mixer speed to medium and beat in the remaining 1 1/3 cups sugar, then the vanilla. Blend in the eggs, one at a time, beating well after adding each one. Beat in the melted chocolate, then the cream, just until completely blended. Don't overmix! Gently spoon the batter on top of the crust.

*3.* Place the cake in a large shallow pan containing hot water that comes about 1 inch up the sides of the springform. Bake until the edges look baked and the center appears set, about 1 1/4 hours. Remove the cake from the water bath, transfer to a wire rack, and let cool for 2 hours (just walk away—don't move it). Leave the cake in the pan, cover loosely with plastic wrap, and refrigerate until completely cold and firm, preferably overnight or at least 4 hours. Transfer to the freezer for 1 hour.

*4.* Meanwhile, set aside 6 of the nicest walnut halves for decorating the center and coarsely chop the rest.

*5.* To make the mirror, combine the caramel topping and corn syrup in a small saucepan over low heat and stir just until spreadable (don't overheat or let boil!). Quickly, spread the caramel over the top of the cold cake (still in the pan). Decorate with a ring of chopped walnuts near the edge and the 6 pretty walnut halves in a star design in the center. Return to the freezer until the mirror sets and is no longer sticky, about 1 hour (do not cover).

*6.* To serve, remove the sides of the springform, leaving the cake on the bottom of the pan. Place on a cake plate and refrigerate until ready to serve. Slice with a sharp straight-edge knife, not a serrated one. Cover any leftover cake and refrigerate or freeze up to 1 month.

*The Junior's Way*

Freeze this cake for 1 hour before spreading the top with the caramel mirror. When warming the caramel ice cream topping, use very low heat and warm it only enough to make it spoonable—no more. If it boils, it might not firm up enough, even when you spread it on the very cold cake. If you can't find caramel ice cream topping, butterscotch or dulce con leche (a milk caramel topping) works well, too.

*"We came up with the idea of adding a chocolate candy bar to our cheesecake,"* said Alan Rosen, *"then covering it with more candies on top. We created a sensation—one that's especially a favorite with our mail-order customers."* Begin with Junior's rich original cheesecake and stir in a large melted bar of Hershey's chocolate. Frost the top and sides with whipped cream chocolate ganache. Then coat the sides with crumbled Heath bars and mound all kinds of chocolate bars on top. Go ahead, have fun—pick the candies you like the best.

# candy bar explosion

**MAKES ONE 9-INCH CHEESECAKE, ABOUT 3 INCHES HIGH**

**FOR THE CRUST:**

1 recipe 9-inch Junior's Sponge Cake Crust (page 17)

Three 1.4-ounce Heath® milk chocolate English toffee candy bars

**FOR THE CHEESECAKE:**

One 8-ounce Hershey's® milk chocolate bar

Four 8-ounce packages cream cheese (use only full fat), at room temperature

1²/₃ cups sugar

¹/₃ cup cornstarch

1 tablespoon pure vanilla extract

2 extra-large eggs

³/₄ cup heavy or whipping cream

**FOR THE TOP DECORATION:**

Four 1.4-ounce Heath milk chocolate English toffee candy bars

1 double recipe Whipped Chocolate Ganache (page 25)

Assorted chocolate candies, such as semisweet chocolate chips, Hershey's Hugs®, Reese's Milk Chocolate Peanut Butter Cups Miniatures®, York® Peppermint Patties (.6 ounce each, halved), Kit Kat® pieces, Hershey's Special Dark Chocolate Nuggets®

*1.* Preheat the oven to 350°F. Generously butter the bottom and sides of a 9-inch springform pan. Wrap the outside with aluminum foil, covering the bottom and extending all the way up the sides. Make and bake the cake crust and leave it in the pan. Keep the oven on. While the crust cools, chop the 3 Heath bars with a chef's knife into small pieces and sprinkle over the cooled cake crust.

*2.* Melt the 8-ounce chocolate bar (page 23) and set aside to cool. Put one package of the cream cheese, ¹/₃ cup of the sugar, and the cornstarch in a large bowl. Beat with an electric mixer on low until creamy, about 3 minutes, scraping down the bowl several times. Blend in the remaining cream cheese, one package at a time, scraping down the bowl after each one. Increase the mixer speed to medium and beat in the remaining 1¹/₃ cups sugar, then the vanilla. Blend in the eggs, one at a time, beating well after adding each one. Beat in the melted chocolate, then the cream, just until completely blended. Don't overmix! Gently spoon the batter over the crust.

*3.* Place the cake in a large shallow pan containing hot water that comes about 1 inch up the sides of the springform. Bake until the edges look baked and the center appears set, about 1¼ hours. Remove the cake from the water bath, transfer to a wire rack, and let cool for 2 hours (just walk away—don't move it). Leave the cake in the pan, cover loosely with plastic wrap, and refrigerate until completely cold, preferably overnight or at least 4 hours. Transfer to the freezer for 1 hour.

*4.* While the cake is in the freezer, chop the 4 Heath bars into chunky, coarse crumbs (these should be a little finer than the ones chopped for the crust, since they need to adhere to the sides of the cake). Make the ganache and refrigerate for at least 1 hour.

*5.* Release and remove the sides of the springform, leaving the cake on the bottom of the pan. Place on a cake plate. Frost the top and sides of the cake with the ganache with a metal spatula. Press the candy crumbs into the sides and arrange the chocolates on the top. Use lots of chocolates, so you completely cover the top of the cake! Refrigerate until ready to serve (do not cover at this stage). Slice with a sharp straight-edge knife, not a serrated one. Cover any left-over cake and refrigerate or freeze up to 1 month.

*The Junior's Way*

Use plenty of chocolates—choose your favorites. Pick different sizes, colors, and shapes: white and dark chocolate kisses; white, butterscotch, and chocolate chips; miniature peanut butter cups; small chocolate bars—some milk or dark chocolate, others with English toffee, almonds or peanuts. I've found that small candies and miniature sizes work best, as you don't have to slice through large pieces of candy when cutting the cake.

*It's no secret: almost everyone loves Heath bars! No wonder—the combination of creamy milk chocolate and brittle English toffee all in one candy is hard to beat. Junior's takes it one step further—they bake crumbled Heath bars inside their chocolate cheesecake, then after baking, crumble even more Heath bars on top. Junior's customers love it—take a taste and you'll quickly see why!*

# heath bar cheesecake

**MAKES ONE 9-INCH CHEESECAKE, ABOUT 2 1/2 INCHES HIGH**

### FOR THE CRUST:

1 recipe 9-inch Dark Chocolate Sponge Cake Crust (page 17)

Three 1.4-ounce Heath® milk chocolate English toffee candy bars

### FOR THE CHEESECAKE:

One 8-ounce Hershey's® milk chocolate bar

Four 8-ounce packages cream cheese (use only full fat), at room temperature

1 2/3 cups sugar

1/3 cup cornstarch

1 tablespoon pure vanilla extract

2 extra-large eggs

3/4 cup heavy or whipping cream

### FOR THE TOPPING:

Five 1.4-ounce Heath milk chocolate English toffee candy bars

Whipped Chocolate Ganache rosettes (page 25; optional)

*1.* Preheat the oven to 350°F. Generously butter the bottom and sides of a 9-inch springform pan. Wrap the outside with aluminum foil, covering the bottom and extending all the way up the sides. Make and bake the cake crust and leave it in the pan. Keep the oven on. While the crust cools, chop 3 Heath bars with a chef's knife into small chunks and sprinkle over the cooled crust.

*2.* Melt the Hershey's bar (page 23) and set aside to cool. Put one package of the cream cheese, 1/3 cup of the sugar, and the cornstarch in a large bowl. Beat with an electric mixer on low until creamy, about 3 minutes, scraping down the bowl several times. Blend in the remaining cream cheese, one package at a time, scraping down the bowl after each one. Increase the mixer speed to medium and beat in the remaining 1 1/3 cups sugar, then the vanilla. Blend in the eggs, one at a time, beating well after adding each one. Blend in the melted chocolate, then the cream, beating just until completely blended. Don't overmix! Gently spoon the batter on top of the crust.

*3.* Place the cake in a large shallow pan containing hot water that comes about 1 inch up the sides of the springform. Bake until the edges look baked and the top of the cake appears set, about 1 1/4 hours. Remove the cake from the water bath, transfer to a wire rack, and let cool for 2 hours (just walk away—don't move it). Leave the cake in the pan, cover loosely with plastic wrap, and refrigerate until completely cold, preferably overnight or at least 4 hours. Transfer to the freezer for 1 hour.

*4.* While the cake is in the freezer, cut 1 Heath bar into 2 equal pieces and reserve one for the center decoration. Chop the remaining 4½ bars for the topping with a chef's knife into small chunks. If you want to decorate with whipped cream rosettes, make the ganache and refrigerate for at least 1 hour.

*5.* To decorate, release and remove the sides of the springform, leaving the cake on the bottom of the pan. Place on a serving plate. Pipe shells or fleur-de-lis of ganache around the bottom edge and top rim of the cake, if you wish. (Use a pastry bag fitted with a medium closed-star tip, #31 or #35.) Sprinkle the candy chunks on top of the cake, covering it almost completely. Decorate the center with the reserved half of the Heath bar. Refrigerate until ready to serve. Slice with a sharp straight-edge knife, not a serrated one. Cover any leftover cake and refrigerate or freeze up to 1 month.

*The Junior's Way*

Chop the candy bars into small chunks with a chef's knife. Don't use a food processor, as that will quickly turn them into fine crumbs.

*This cheesecake gets its name and its toppings from the popular rocky road ice cream and candy, which became all the rage in the mid-1900s— especially among the after-school crowd at hometown ice cream parlors throughout America. The deep dark chocolate, marshmallows, and nuts are all here. The original ice cream contained almonds, but you can use any nut you want. Junior's likes peanuts the best!*

# rocky road

**MAKES ONE 9-INCH CHEESECAKE, ABOUT 2 1/2 INCHES HIGH**

1 recipe 9-inch Dark Chocolate Sponge Cake Crust (page 17)

**FOR THE CHEESECAKE:**

8 ounces bittersweet or semisweet chocolate

Three 8-ounce packages cream cheese (use only full fat), at room temperature

1 1/3 cups sugar

1/4 cup cornstarch

1 tablespoon pure vanilla extract

2 extra-large eggs

3/4 cup heavy or whipping cream

3/4 cup dry-roasted peanuts (preferably unsalted), coarsely chopped

**FOR THE ROCKY ROAD TOPPING:**

One 7.5-ounce jar Marshmallow Fluff®

1 cup miniature marshmallows

1/4 cup whole dry-roasted (preferably unsalted) peanuts

2 ounces bittersweet or semisweet chocolate, melted (page 23)

*1.* Preheat the oven to 350°F. Generously butter the bottom and sides of a 9-inch springform pan. Wrap the outside with aluminum foil, covering the bottom and extending all the way up the sides. Make and bake the cake crust and leave it in the pan. Keep the oven on.

*2.* Melt the 8 ounces chocolate (page 23) and set aside to cool. Put one package of the cream cheese, 1/3 cup of the sugar, and the cornstarch in a large bowl. Beat with an electric mixer on low until creamy, about 3 minutes, scraping down the bowl several times. Blend in the remaining cream cheese, one package at a time, scraping down the bowl after each one. Increase the mixer speed to medium and beat in the remaining 1 cup sugar, then the vanilla. Blend in the eggs, one at a time, beating well after adding each one. Beat in the melted chocolate, then the cream, just until completely blended. Don't overmix! Stir in the chopped peanuts. Gently spoon the batter on top of the crust.

*3.* Place the cake in a large shallow pan containing hot water that comes about 1 inch up the sides of the springform. Bake until the edges look baked and the top of the cake appears set, about 1 1/4 hours. Remove the cake from the water bath, transfer to a wire rack, and let cool for 2 hours (just walk away—don't move it). Leave the cake in the pan, cover loosely with plastic wrap, and refrigerate until cold, preferably overnight or at least 4 hours.

*4.* To serve, release and remove the sides of the springform, leaving the cake on the bottom. Place on a cake plate. Spread the Marshmallow Fluff over the top and down the sides—but stop before covering the sides completely. Be sure to leave some of the chocolate peeking out near the bottom. Scatter the marshmallows on it, then the whole peanuts. Fit a pastry bag with a small round tip (#2 or #3), spoon in the melted chocolate, and pipe continuous swirls of lines on top, making the lines about ⅜ inch apart. Refrigerate until ready to serve. Slice with a sharp straight-edge knife, not a serrated one. If there's any cake left, cover it and refrigerate, or wrap and freeze for up to 1 month.

## The Junior's Way

If you can find miniature marshmallows, buy them to decorate this cake. But if they're not available, purchase the larger marshmallows instead. Cut them into ½-inch cubes with sharp kitchen shears. To prevent the marshmallows from sticking to the scissors, dust the blades with cornstarch frequently.

*This cake combines bites of dough inside the famous cheesecake with tiny baked cookies as decorations. Guaranteed to be a winner! Baker's Tip: If you want lots of extra cookies to eat, just double the cookie dough recipe.*

# chocolate chip cookie dough cheesecake

**MAKES ONE 9-INCH CHEESECAKE, ABOUT 2½ INCHES HIGH**

**FOR THE CHOCOLATE CHIP COOKIE DOUGH:**

⅔ cup cake flour

½ cup all-purpose flour

½ teaspoon baking soda

½ teaspoon salt

½ cup (1 stick) unsalted butter, at room temperature

½ cup granulated sugar

¼ cup firmly packed light brown sugar

1 extra-large egg

1 teaspoon pure vanilla extract

1 cup mini chocolate chips

⅓ cup finely chopped pecans

*1.* Make the cookie dough. Combine both flours, the baking soda, and salt in a medium-size bowl and set aside. Cream the butter in a large bowl with an electric mixer on high for 2 minutes. With the mixer still running, gradually add both sugars, then the egg. Continue beating until the mixture is creamy and light yellow, then beat in the vanilla. With a wooden spoon, stir in the flour mixture just until mixed (do not overmix the batter or the cookies could become tough). Stir in the chocolate chips and pecans. Transfer 1 cup of dough to a small bowl (to drop into the cake batter). The rest of the dough will be baked into cookies later. Refrigerate both portions of dough.

*2.* Make and bake the brownie crust, then transfer to a wire rack to cool (do not remove the crust from the pan). Keep the oven on.

*3.* Make the cheesecake filling. Put one package of the cream cheese, ⅓ cup of the sugar, and the cornstarch in a large bowl and beat with an electric mixer on low until creamy, about 3 minutes, scraping down the bowl several times. Blend in the remaining packages of cream cheese one package at a time, scraping down the bowl after each one. Increase the mixer speed to medium and beat in the remaining 1⅓ cups sugar, then the vanilla. Blend in the eggs, one at a time, beating well after adding each one. Beat in the cream just until completely blended. Don't overmix!

**FOR THE BROWNIE CRUST:**
1 recipe 9-inch Brownie Shortbread Cookie Crust (page 20)

**FOR THE CHEESECAKE:**
Four 8-ounce packages cream cheese (use only full fat), at room temperature

1 2/3 cups sugar

1/4 cup cornstarch

1 tablespoon pure vanilla extract

2 extra-large eggs

3/4 cup heavy or whipping cream

**FOR THE TOPPING:**
1 recipe Whipped Chocolate Ganache (page 25)

*The Junior's Way*

To ensure that the cookie dough does not sink to the bottom of the cake, use mini chocolate chips, not the larger ones, and chop the pecans into small pieces. Also, be sure to drop very small amounts of dough into the batter—only 1/2 teaspoon.

*4.* Spread half the cheesecake batter on top of the brownie crust in the springform. Using half of the 1 cup reserved cookie dough, drop 1/2 teaspoonfuls on top of the filling. Cover with the rest of the batter and drop the remaining 1/2 cup cookie dough on top, again in 1/2 teaspoonfuls. Using a small spoon, gently push down the bits of dough, letting them peek through the batter a little.

*5.* Place the cake in a large shallow pan containing hot water that comes about 1 inch up the sides of the springform. Bake until the edges are light golden brown and the top of the cake is slightly golden tan, about 1¼ hours. Remove the cake from the water bath, transfer to a wire rack, and let cool for 2 hours (just walk away—don't move it). Leave the cake in the pan, cover loosely with plastic wrap, and refrigerate preferably overnight or at least 4 hours. Transfer to the freezer for 1 hour.

*6.* Meanwhile, make the chocolate ganache. Refrigerate at least 1 hour.

*7.* While the ganache chills, bake the remaining cookie dough. Preheat the oven to 375°F. Line 2 baking sheets with parchment paper or butter them. Drop the dough by level teaspoonfuls onto the sheets, about 2 inches apart (you will have about 50 small cookies about 1½ inches in diameter). Bake the cookies until golden and almost firm, 9 to 11 minutes (watch carefully and don't let them get too brown). Let cool on the pan for 10 minutes, then slide them off the sheets onto a baking rack to cool.

*8.* To decorate the cake, release and remove the sides of the springform, leaving the cake on the bottom. Place on a cake plate (use one that can go into the freezer). While the cake is still very cold, decorate the sides and the top of the cake with the ganache (since the cake is icy cold, it's easy to swirl the ganache into decorative peaks). Leave a 3-inch circle of cheesecake unfrosted in the center so the white cheesecake is peeking through. Break a few cookies into small irregular pieces and mound them around the top edge of the cake, then decorate with a few whole cookies in the center. (Store the rest of the cookies in an airtight cookie jar or freeze for enjoying later.) Return the cake to the freezer for 1 hour to set the ganache, then transfer to the refrigerator until ready to serve. Slice with a sharp straight-edge knife, not a serrated one. Cover any leftover cake and refrigerate or freeze up to 1 month.

# Little Fellas

Junior's regular customers know these Little Fellas well. They're one of the best-selling cheesecakes at the Junior's bakery in Grand Central Station in Manhattan. Anytime you're flying through the station to catch a train, you can grab one of these delicious little gems at the bakery or at the restaurant's "to go" counter, down near the tracks. Choose from three flavors: plain, chocolate swirl, or raspberry swirl. Each is packed ready-to-go and small enough for you to eat the whole little cake at one time. We've created more Little Fellas in other fabulous flavors: cappuccino, Key lime, and peaches & cream. They're faster to make than Junior's original cheesecake, because most are all filling, no crust. Alan Rosen suggests, "Bake a double recipe of any of them — they freeze well, making them the perfect instant dessert. Just defrost and serve."

*Just what you'd expect: Junior's original cheesecake in a delicious small package.*

# original little fella cheesecake

Two 8-ounce packages
cream cheese (use only full fat),
at room temperature

¾ cup sugar

2 tablespoons cornstarch

1 tablespoon pure vanilla extract

2 extra-large eggs

⅓ cup heavy or whipping cream

12 small fresh strawberries
or raspberries (optional)

1 recipe Junior's Signature
Strawberry Sauce
(optional, page 31)

**The Junior's Way**

Master Baker Michael Goodman explains: "We use reusable silicone cupcake muffin pans for baking these Little Fellas. We bake them, then cool and freeze them in the same pans. The frozen little cakes pop right out!" You can find silicone muffin pans in bright colors in cookware stores or on the web. You can also buy reusable opaque silicone liners for your metal muffin pan or use disposable foil, parchment, or paper liners.

**MAKES ONE DOZEN LITTLE FELLAS**

*1.* Preheat the oven to 350°F. Line 12 muffin cups with silicone, foil, parchment, or paper liners.

*2.* Put one package of the cream cheese, ¼ cup of the sugar, and the cornstarch in a large bowl. Beat with an electric mixer on low until creamy, about 3 minutes, scraping down the bowl a few times. Blend in the remaining package of cream cheese. Increase the mixer speed to medium and beat in the remaining ½ cup sugar, then the vanilla. Blend in the eggs, one at a time, beating well after adding each one. Beat in the cream just until it's completely blended. Be careful not to overmix!

*3.* Divide the batter among the 12 muffin cups (fill each one almost up to the top). Place the muffin tin in a large shallow pan, then add hot water so it comes about 1 inch up the sides of the tin. Bake the cakes until set and the centers are slightly puffy and golden, about 45 minutes. Remove the cakes from the water bath, transfer the tin to a wire rack, and let cool for 2 hours. Cover the cakes with plastic wrap (do not remove from the tin) and put in the freezer until cold, at least 1 hour.

*4.* To remove the cakes, lift them out of the cups with your hands and peel off the liners. Place the cakes, top side down, on a serving platter or individual dessert plates and refrigerate until ready to serve. Top each with a strawberry and serve drizzled with sauce, if you wish. If there are any cakes left, cover with plastic wrap and store in the refrigerator. Or remove the berries, then wrap and freeze for up to 1 month.

*Here's another winning Little Fella—this one made with the original cheesecake batter, then swirled throughout with chocolate.*

# little fella chocolate swirls

**MAKES ONE DOZEN LITTLE FELLAS**

Two 8-ounce packages cream cheese (use only full fat), at room temperature

2/3 cup sugar

2 tablespoons cornstarch

1 tablespoon pure vanilla extract

2 extra-large eggs

1/2 cup heavy or whipping cream

1 1/2 tablespoons unsweetened cocoa powder

1 recipe Chocolate Curls (optional, page 21)

One 12-ounce jar hot fudge ice cream topping (optional), warmed

*1.* Preheat the oven to 350°F. Line 12 standard muffin cups with silicone, foil, parchment, or paper liners.

*2.* Put one package of the cream cheese, 1/3 cup of the sugar, and the cornstarch in a large bowl. Beat with an electric mixer on low until creamy, about 3 minutes, scraping down the bowl a few times. Blend in the remaining package of cream cheese. Increase the mixer speed to medium and beat in the remaining 1/3 cup sugar, then the vanilla. Blend in the eggs, one at a time, beating well after adding each one. Beat in the cream just until it's completely blended. Be careful not to overmix! Remove 3/4 cup of the batter and stir in the cocoa.

*3.* Divide the white batter among the 12 muffin cups. Drop a heaping teaspoon of the chocolate batter in the center of each, pushing it down slightly. Using a small knife, cut through the batter just until dark swirls appear.

*4.* Place the muffin tin in a large shallow pan and add hot water until it comes about 1 inch up the sides of the tin. Bake the cakes until set and slightly puffy, about 45 minutes. Remove the cakes from the water bath, transfer the tin to a wire rack, and let cool for 2 hours. Cover the cakes with plastic wrap (do not remove from the tin) and put in the freezer until cold, at least 1 hour.

*5.* To remove the cakes, lift them out with your hands and peel off the liners. Place the cakes, top side up, on a serving platter or individual dessert plates. Top with the chocolate curls if you wish and refrigerate. Serve drizzled with the hot fudge sauce, if you wish. If there are any cakes left, cover with plastic wrap and store in the refrigerator or wrap and freeze for up to 1 month.

*These little cakes with red swirls taste like they were made with fresh raspberries. Actually they are made with frozen berries, just like at Junior's. You don't need to worry about overripe berries or fluctuating high market prices of the fresh ones. Just defrost the frozen berries and purée them— no straining needed!*

# little fella
# raspberry swirls

### MAKES 13 LITTLE FELLAS

6 ounces (about ²/₃ cup) dry-pack frozen whole raspberries (unsweetened, not in syrup), thawed and drained well

Two 8-ounce packages cream cheese (use only full fat), at room temperature

²/₃ cup sugar

3 tablespoons cornstarch

1 tablespoon pure vanilla extract

2 extra-large eggs

¹/₂ cup heavy or whipping cream

13 fresh raspberries (large, pretty ones)

*front to back*
Little Fella Chocolate Swirl topped with chocolate curls (page 133) and Little Fella Raspberry Swirl with fresh raspberries.

*1.* Preheat the oven to 350°F. Line 13 standard muffin cups with silicone, foil, parchment, or paper liners. (If you have only 12, use a custard cup for the thirteenth one.)

*2.* Pulse the thawed raspberries in your food processor until smooth (you need ¹/₃ cup of purée). Set aside.

*3.* Put one package of the cream cheese, ¹/₃ cup of the sugar, and the cornstarch in a large bowl. Beat with an electric mixer on low until creamy, about 3 minutes, scraping down the bowl a few times. Blend in the remaining package of cream cheese. Increase the mixer speed to medium and beat in the remaining ¹/₃ cup sugar, then the vanilla. Blend in the eggs, one at a time, beating well after adding each one. Beat in the cream just until it's completely blended. Be careful not to overmix!

*4.* Divide the batter among the 13 muffin cups (fill each one almost up to the top). Drop a heaping teaspoon of the raspberry purée in the center of each cup, pushing it down slightly into each little cake as you go. Using a thin, pointed knife, cut through the batter a few times, just until raspberry swirls appear (do not mix in the purée completely or the cakes will turn pink and the swirls will disappear).

*5.* Place the muffin tin in a large shallow pan and pour hot water in until it comes about 1 inch up the sides of the tin. Bake the cakes until set and the centers are slightly puffy and golden with red raspberry swirls, about 45 minutes. Remove the cakes from the water bath, transfer the tin to a wire rack, and let cool for 2 hours. Cover the cakes with plastic wrap (do not remove from the tin) and put in the freezer until cold, at least 1 hour.

*6.* To remove the cakes, lift them out the cups with your hands and peel off the liners. Place the cakes, top side up, on a serving platter or individual dessert plates. Top each with a raspberry and refrigerate until ready to serve. If there are any cakes left, cover with plastic wrap and store in the refrigerator. Or remove the fresh berries, then wrap and freeze for up to 1 month.

## The Junior's Way

Junior's Master Baker Michael Goodman says, "Cheesecake is more like a custard than a cake. So you're not really baking it, you're cooking it." This is the reason that a medium moist heat (not a high dry one) works best, especially on these Little Fellas.

*These little cakes are exactly like Junior's Strawberry Swirl Cheesecake—just smaller. It's the same original cheesecake filling they began baking in the 1950s—there's just less of it in each cake.*

# little fella strawberry swirls

**MAKES 13 LITTLE FELLAS**

6 ounces (about ⅔ cup) dry-pack frozen whole strawberries (unsweetened, not in syrup), thawed and drained well

Two 8-ounce packages cream cheese (use only full fat), at room temperature

⅔ cup sugar

3 tablespoons cornstarch

1 tablespoon pure vanilla extract

2 extra-large eggs

½ cup heavy or whipping cream

1 recipe Junior's Signature Strawberry Sauce (optional, page 31)

*1.* Preheat the oven to 350°F. Line 13 standard muffin cups with silicone, foil, parchment, or paper liners. (If you have only 12, use a custard cup for the thirteenth one.)

*2.* Pulse the thawed strawberries in your food processor until smooth (you need ⅓ cup of purée). Set aside.

*3.* Put one package of the cream cheese, ⅓ cup of the sugar, and the cornstarch in a large bowl. Beat with an electric mixer on low until creamy, about 3 minutes, scraping down the bowl a few times. Blend in the remaining package of cream cheese. Increase the mixer speed to medium and beat in the remaining ⅓ cup sugar, then the vanilla. Blend in the eggs, one at a time, beating well after adding each one. Beat in the cream just until it's completely blended. Be careful not to overmix!

*4.* Divide the batter among the 13 muffin cups. Drop a heaping teaspoon of the purée in the center of each cup, pushing it down slightly into each little cake as you go. Using a small knife, cut through the batter a few times, just until pink swirls appear (do not mix in the purée completely or the cakes will turn pink and the swirls will disappear). Place the muffin tin in a large shallow pan and add hot water until it comes about 1 inch up the sides of the tin.

*5.* Bake the cakes until set and the centers are slightly puffy and golden with red strawberry swirls, about 45 minutes. Remove the cakes from the water bath, transfer the tin to a wire rack, and let cool for 2 hours. Cover the cakes with plastic wrap (do not remove from the tin) and put in the freezer until cold, at least 1 hour. In the meantime, make the strawberry sauce if you wish.

*6.* To remove the cakes, lift them out of the cups with your hands and peel off the liners. Place the cakes, top side up, on a serving platter or individual dessert plates and refrigerate until ready to serve. If desired, spoon a heaping spoonful of sauce over each. If there are any cakes left, cover with plastic wrap and store in the refrigerator, or wrap and freeze for up to 1 month.

*The Junior's Way*

Use the tip of a small, thin paring knife to swirl in the strawberry purée. This gives the delicate swirls of the intertwining red and white batters that you need in such small cakes.

*For your next dinner party, skip the process of making cappuccino after dinner and serve these Little Fellas instead. They're flavored with instant espresso, then topped the traditional Italian way with chocolate curls and the finest dusting of cocoa. Tre bellissimo!*

# cappuccino little fellas

**MAKES ONE DOZEN LITTLE FELLAS**

1 tablespoon instant freeze-dried espresso or instant coffee

1 tablespoon hot water

Two 8-ounce packages cream cheese (use only full fat), at room temperature

$2/3$ cup sugar

3 tablespoons cornstarch

1 tablespoon pure vanilla extract

2 extra-large eggs

$1/2$ cup heavy or whipping cream

1 recipe Chocolate Curls (page 21)

1 tablespoon unsweetened cocoa powder

*1.* Preheat the oven to 350°F. Line 12 standard muffin cups with silicone, foil, parchment, or paper liners. Dissolve the instant espresso in the hot water in a small cup and let stand.

*2.* Put one package of the cream cheese, $1/3$ cup of the sugar, and the cornstarch in a large bowl. Beat with an electric mixer on low until creamy, about 3 minutes, scraping down the bowl a few times. Blend in the remaining package of cream cheese. Increase the mixer speed to medium and beat in the remaining $1/3$ cup sugar, then the vanilla. Add the eggs, one at a time, beating well after each one. Stir the dissolved coffee into the cream and beat into the cream cheese mixture just until it's completely blended. Be careful not to overmix!

*3.* Divide the batter among the 12 muffin cups. Place the muffin tin in a large shallow pan containing hot water that comes about 1 inch up the sides of the tin. Bake the cakes until set and the centers are slightly puffy and golden, about 45 minutes. Remove the cakes from the water bath, transfer the tin to a wire rack, and let cool for 2 hours. Cover the cakes with plastic wrap (do not remove from the pan) and place in the freezer until cold, at least 1 hour.

*4.* To remove the cakes, lift them out of the cups with your hands and peel off the liners. Place the cakes, top side down, on a serving platter or individual dessert plates. Sprinkle each cake with chocolate curls and dust with a little cocoa. Refrigerate until ready to serve. If there are any cakes left, cover with plastic wrap and store in the refrigerator or wrap and freeze for up to 1 month.

*You know when it's summertime at Junior's, because fresh peach pie is on the menu. These Little Fellas bring back those summer memories, all year long. For a fancy touch, pipe each with a whipped cream rosette and a little peach slice. For a more totable topping, use Junior's Cinnamon Crumb Topping (page 29), similar to those that often appear on fresh peach pies.*

# peaches & cream little fellas

**MAKES 13 LITTLE FELLAS**

8 ounces (about ¾ cup) dry-pack frozen peaches (unsweetened, not in syrup), thawed and drained well, plus a few extra peach slices for decorating

3 tablespoons cornstarch

Two 8-ounce packages cream cheese (use only full fat), at room temperature

²⁄₃ cup sugar

1 tablespoon pure vanilla extract

2 extra-large eggs

½ cup heavy or whipping cream

1 drop orange food coloring (optional)

1 recipe Decorator's Whipped Cream (page 26), refrigerated at least 30 minutes

13 small fresh peach slices

*1.* Preheat the oven to 350°F. Line 13 standard muffin cups with silicone, foil, parchment, or paper liners. (If you have only 12, use a custard cup for the thirteenth one.)

*2.* Pulse the peaches in your food processor until smooth (you need ½ cup of purée). Stir in 1 tablespoon of the cornstarch and set aside. It will thicken slightly as it stands.

*3.* Put one package of the cream cheese, ⅓ cup of the sugar, and the remaining 2 tablespoons cornstarch in a large bowl. Beat with an electric mixer on low until creamy, about 3 minutes, scraping down the bowl a few times. Beat in the remaining package of cream cheese. Increase the mixer speed to medium and beat in the remaining ⅓ cup sugar, then the vanilla. Blend in the eggs, one at a time, beating well after adding each one. Beat in the cream just until it's completely blended. Be careful not to overmix! Blend in the peach purée. Add a drop or two or orange food coloring, if you wish.

*4.* Divide the batter among the 13 muffin cups. Place the muffin tin in a large shallow pan and add hot water until it comes about 1 inch up the sides of the tin. Bake the cakes until set and the centers are slightly puffy and golden, about 45 minutes. Remove the cakes from the water bath, transfer the tin to a wire rack, and let cool for 2 hours. Cover the cakes with plastic wrap (do not remove from the pan) and put in the freezer until cold, at least 1 hour.

*5.* To remove the cakes, lift them out of the cups with your hands and peel off the liners. Place the cakes, top side down, on a serving platter or individual dessert plates. Fit a pastry bag with a medium closed-star tip (#31), fill it with the whipped cream, and pipe a pyramid of swirls and rosettes on top of each, topping each off with a tiny "star" rosette (page 26). Top each with a small peach slice. Refrigerate until ready to serve. If there are any cakes left, remove the fruits, cover the cakes with plastic wrap, and store in the refrigerator, or wrap and freeze for up to 1 month.

*The Junior's Way*

**Purées of frozen fruits work the best in these little cakes. These purées make them taste like the real thing—without the time and hassle of peeling and chopping fresh fruit.**

*There seems to always be another Key lime recipe to try, and this one is worth pulling out the muffin tin for! It's a small size of the original cheesecake crowned with a party-perfect topping of delicious lime mousse that tastes surprisingly like the traditional Key lime pie filling. The authentic Key lime pie recipe does not add color to the lime filling. Junior's doesn't either, but if you want a hint of a greenish tint, add 1 or 2 drops of green food coloring— no more! Go ahead and double the recipe—these little cakes freeze well.*

# key lime
# little fellas

**MAKES ONE DOZEN LITTLE FELLAS**

### FOR THE CHEESECAKES:
Two 8-ounce packages
cream cheese (use only full fat),
at room temperature

¾ cup sugar

3 tablespoons cornstarch

1 tablespoon pure vanilla extract

2 extra-large eggs

⅓ cup heavy or whipping cream

1 teaspoon grated lime rind

### FOR THE LIME MOUSSE:
1 recipe Decorator's
Whipped Cream (page 26)

¼ cup frozen limeade concentrate,
thawed just until spoonable

1 to 2 drops green food coloring
(optional)

*1.* Preheat the oven to 350°F. Line 12 standard muffin cups with silicone, foil, parchment, or paper liners.

*2.* Put one package of the cream cheese, ¼ cup of the sugar, and the cornstarch in a large bowl. Beat with an electric mixer on low until creamy, about 3 minutes, scraping down the bowl a few times. Blend in the remaining package of cream cheese. Increase the mixer speed to medium and beat in the remaining ½ cup sugar, then the vanilla. Blend in the eggs, one at a time, beating well after adding each one. Beat in the cream just until it's completely blended. Be careful not to overmix! Stir in the lime rind.

*3.* Divide the batter among the 12 muffin cups. Place the muffin tin in a large shallow pan and add hot water until it comes about 1 inch up the sides of the tin. Bake the cakes until set and the centers are slightly puffy and golden, about 45 minutes. Remove the cakes from the water bath, transfer the tin to a wire rack, and let cool for 2 hours. Cover the cakes with plastic wrap (do not remove from the pan) and put in the freezer until cold, or at least 1 hour. Don't worry if they settle a little in the center; you'll be filling it with lime mousse.

*4.* To remove the cakes, lift them out of the cups with your hands and peel off the liners. Place the cakes, top side up, on a serving platter or individual dessert plates.

*5.* To make the lime mousse, make the Decorator's Whip Cream, then stir in the limeade concentrate (it's best if it's still slightly frozen). Add the food coloring if you wish. Refrigerate for 30 minutes. Fit a pastry bag with a medium closed-star tip (#31) or a medium open-star tip (#32), pack it with the lime mousse, and pipe the lime mousse on top of each Little Fella, finishing each off with a "star" rosette on top (page 26). Refrigerate until ready to serve. If there are any cakes left, cover with plastic wrap and store in the refrigerator, or wrap and freeze for up to 1 month.

## The Junior's Way

If you haven't the time for piping the decorations, here's a fast and easy way to top these Little Fellas: Place about 2 tablespoonfuls of lime mousse in the center of each little cake. Using the small pointed end of a paring knife, make deep swirls in the mousse, finishing each off in a high peak in the center. Swirl the cake in your hand as you work and leave about 1/2 inch of the cake showing around the edge. For an added touch, shower the mousse with a little green decorating sugar or multicolored sprinkles, if you like. Look for them at a gourmet cookshop, in the baking aisle of your supermarket, or on an Internet bakeware site.

*These are exactly what they sound like: All of the goodness found in Junior's carrot cake and their famous cheesecake stacked up into individual Little Fellas. They're decorative enough for the fanciest dinner party, and yummy enough to want them on hand all the time—store the extras in the freezer for when the hankering hits.*

# carrot cake little fellas

## FOR THE CARROT CAKE CRUST:

1/2 cup all-purpose flour

1/2 teaspoon baking powder

1/2 teaspoon ground cinnamon

1/4 teaspoon salt

1/8 teaspoon baking soda

1 extra-large egg

1/2 cup granulated sugar

1/4 cup vegetable oil

1 tablespoon heavy or whipping cream

1/2 teaspoon pure vanilla extract

3 large carrots, finely grated (1 1/2 cups)

1/3 cup peeled, cored, and minced apple

1/4 cup finely chopped walnuts

## FOR THE CHEESECAKE:

Two 8-ounce packages cream cheese (use only full fat), at room temperature

3/4 cup granulated sugar

2 tablespoons cornstarch

1 tablespoon pure vanilla extract

2 extra-large eggs

1/3 cup heavy or whipping cream

*(continued on page 147)*

**MAKES TWO DOZEN LITTLE FELLAS**

*1.* Preheat the oven to 350°F. Line 24 standard muffin cups with silicone, foil, or paper liners.

*2.* Make the carrot cake crust. Sift the flour, baking powder, cinnamon, salt, and baking soda together in a medium-size bowl and set aside. Beat the egg in a large bowl with an electric mixer on high until light yellow, about 3 minutes. With the mixer still running, gradually add the granulated sugar. Now, slowly drizzle in the oil, then the cream and vanilla. When the batter is light golden and airy, it's ready (this usually takes a total of 15 to 20 minutes of beating). Stir in the flour mixture with a wooden spoon, then stir in the carrots, apple, and walnuts. Divide the batter evenly among the 24 muffin cups (you'll need about 1 heaping tablespoon in each), then bake until the center springs back when lightly touched, about 20 minutes. Do not overbake! Remove the tins from the oven. Leave the oven on.

*3.* Make the cheesecake filling. Put one package of the cream cheese, 1/4 cup of the granulated sugar, and the cornstarch in a large bowl. Beat with an electric mixer on low until creamy, about 3 minutes, scraping down the bowl a few times. Blend in the remaining package of cream cheese. Increase the mixer speed to medium and beat in the remaining 1/2 cup granulated sugar, then the vanilla. Blend in the eggs, one at a time, beating well after adding each one. Blend in the cream and vanilla just until completely blended. Be careful not to overmix!

**FOR THE CREAM CHEESE
FROSTING AND TOPPING:**

3/4 cup (1 1/2 sticks) unsalted butter,
at room temperature

Two 8-ounce packages
cream cheese (use only full fat),
at room temperature

4 cups sifted confectioners' sugar

2 teaspoons pure vanilla extract

3 tablespoons heavy
or whipping cream

Divide the batter among the 24 muffin cups, spooning it gently on top of each carrot cake crust. Place the muffin tins in a large shallow pan and add hot water until it comes about 1 inch up the sides of the tins.

*4.* Bake the cakes until set and the centers are slightly puffy and golden, about 45 minutes. Remove the cakes from the water bath, transfer the tin to a wire rack, and let cool for 2 hours. Cover the cakes with plastic wrap (do not remove from the pan) and put in the freezer until cold, at least 1 hour.

*5.* To remove the cakes, lift out the cakes with your hands and peel off the liners. Place the cakes, top side down, on a serving platter or individual dessert plates.

*6.* Whip up the frosting. Cream the butter and cream cheese together in a medium-size bowl with the mixer on high speed. Beat in the confectioners' sugar until smooth. Beat in the vanilla. With the mixer running, gradually add the cream and beat until the frosting looks whipped and creamy. Fit a pastry bag with a medium closed-star tip (#31) or a medium open-star tip (#32), spoon the frosting into it, and pipe small rosettes on top of each little cake. Finish off with a star in the center, ending in a peak (page 26). Refrigerate until ready to serve. If there are any cakes left, cover with plastic wrap and store in the refrigerator, or wrap and freeze for up to 1 month.

## *The Junior's Way*

If the frosting softens while you're piping it onto the little cakes, place the pastry bag in the freezer for about 15 minutes—just until the bag feels cold to your hands again. The frosting needs to be cold to pipe the best rosettes.

# Skyscraper Cheesecakes

Just when you thought Junior's couldn't get any better, the bakers created something new: a cake within a cake. They start with layers of homemade traditional cake, then enhance them with an extra thick creamy layer of Junior's Original New York Cheesecake. The cakes are held together and iced with one of Junior's delicious icings. These creations are towering confections of unparalleled lusciousness. We call them (appropriately!) Skyscraper Cheesecakes.

Skyscrapers are two-day affairs. The cheesecake is baked the first day and frozen overnight, then put together with the cake layers the following day. But, believe us, they're worth every minute when you hear the delighted gasps from your astonished guests.

*The 1950s' dinner menu for the opening of Junior's restaurant included twenty-nine dessert choices. Most came free with the complete dinner, but not the Fresh Strawberry Shortcake with Fresh Strawberry Sauce. You had to pay an extra 35 cents for that irresistible offering. Now, that same shortcake has grown bigger and better: layers of homemade sponge cake laced with thick layers of strawberry cheesecake—all put together with whipped cream and lots of fresh berries.*

# strawberry shortcake cheesecake

**FOR THE CHEESECAKE LAYER:**

10 ounces (about 1 cup) dry-pack frozen whole strawberries (unsweetened, not in syrup), thawed and drained well

$1/3$ cup plus 1 teaspoon cornstarch

Three 8-ounce packages cream cheese (use only full fat), at room temperature

$1\,1/3$ cups sugar

1 tablespoon pure vanilla extract

2 extra-large eggs

$2/3$ cup heavy or whipping cream

3 to 4 drops red food coloring (optional)

**FOR THE SPONGE CAKE (2 LAYERS):**

$2/3$ cup sifted cake flour

$1\,1/2$ teaspoons baking powder

$1/2$ teaspoon salt

5 extra-large eggs, separated

$2/3$ cup sugar

$1\,1/2$ teaspoons pure vanilla extract

$1/4$ teaspoon pure lemon extract

$1/4$ cup ($1/2$ stick) unsalted butter, melted

$1/2$ teaspoon cream of tartar

*(continued on page 152)*

**MAKES ONE 9-INCH THREE-LAYER CAKE, ABOUT 5 INCHES HIGH**

*1.* Preheat the oven to 350°F. Generously butter the bottom and sides of one 9-inch springform pan and two 9-inch round layer cake pans. Wrap the outside of the springform (but not the cake pans) with aluminum foil, covering the bottom and extending all the way up the sides. *Very important:* Line the bottom of all three pans with parchment or waxed paper (do not let the paper come up the sides).

*2.* Pulse the thawed strawberries in your food processor until smooth (you need ¾ cup of purée). Stir in the 1 teaspoon of cornstarch and set aside. It will thicken slightly as it stands.

*3.* Put one package of the cream cheese, ⅓ cup of the sugar, and the cornstarch in a large bowl. Beat with an electric mixer on low until creamy, about 3 minutes, scraping down the bowl a few times. Beat in the remaining cream cheese, one package at a time, scraping down the bowl after each. Increase the mixer speed to medium and beat in the remaining 1 cup sugar, then the vanilla. Blend in the eggs, one at a time, beating well after adding each. Beat in the

**TO ASSEMBLE AND FROST:**

2 quarts fresh strawberries

1 tablespoon unflavored granulated gelatin

3 tablespoons cold water

1 quart heavy or whipping cream

⅓ cup sugar

1 tablespoon pure vanilla extract

cream just until it's completely blended. Be careful not to overmix! Fold in the strawberry purée, plus the food coloring, if you wish (use just enough to tint the batter light pink).

*4.* Gently spoon the batter into the springform, then place it in a large shallow pan containing hot water that comes about 1 inch up the sides of the spring-form. Bake the cake until the edges are light golden brown and the top is set, about 1¼ hours. Remove the cake from the water bath, transfer the tin to a wire rack, and let cool in the pan for 2 hours, then cover with plastic wrap and refrigerate until completely cold, about 4 hours. Then freeze overnight and/or until ready to assemble the cake.

*5.* While the cheesecake is cooling, make the sponge cake layers. Check that the oven is preheated to 350°F and that the water bath has been removed. In a small bowl, sift the flour, baking powder, and salt together. Beat the egg yolks in a large bowl with an electric mixer on high for 3 minutes. While the mixer is still running, slowly add ⅓ cup of the sugar and continue beating until thick, light yellow ribbons form in the bowl, about 5 minutes more. Beat in the extracts. Sift the flour mixture over the batter and stir it in by hand, just until no white flecks are visible. Blend in the melted butter.

*6.* Put the egg whites and cream of tartar in a clean medium-size bowl and, using clean, dry beaters, beat with the mixer on high until frothy. Gradually add the remaining ⅓ cup sugar and continue beating until stiff peaks form (the whites will stand up and look glossy, not dry). Fold about one-third of the whites into the batter, then add the remaining whites. Don't worry if you still see a few white specks—they'll disappear during baking. Divide the batter evenly between the two layer cake pans and bake until golden (not wet or sticky) and the centers spring back when lightly pressed, about 12 minutes. Let the cakes cool in the pan on a wire rack for 15 minutes, then turn them out onto the rack and gently peel off the paper liners. Let cool completely, then cover with plastic wrap and refrigerate overnight or until ready to assemble the cake.

*7.* On the day you plan to assemble the cake, hull 1 quart of the strawberries, then cut them into ½-inch pieces (you need 2 cups). Reserve the remaining berries for decorating the cake.

8. Make the frosting. Place the gelatin in a heatproof measuring cup, stir in the cold water, and let stand until it swells and thickens. Cook in the microwave on high for about 30 seconds or over a pan of simmering water for about 1 minute, until clear and completely melted. In a medium-size bowl, whip the cream with an electric mixer on high until it thickens and soft peaks just begin to form. With the mixer still running, add the sugar and beat just until the cream stands up in peaks (don't overmix or the cream will curdle). Beat in the vanilla. Add the melted gelatin all at once and beat until thoroughly incorporated. Refrigerate the cream for at least 30 minutes (preferably no longer than 1 hour) in two bowls: 2 cups in a small bowl for piping decorations on the top of the cake and the remainder in a second larger bowl for frosting the cake. Meanwhile, remove the frozen strawberry cheesecake from the freezer and let stand at room temperature for 10 minutes.

9. Place one layer of sponge cake, top side down, on a cake plate. Spread evenly with a thin layer of whipped cream frosting from the large bowl and half of the strawberry pieces. Release and remove the ring of the springform, then remove the frozen cheesecake from the bottom of the pan (see Solution on page 14). Peel away the paper liner and place top side down on top of the frosted bottom layer. Press the cheesecake down gently, just enough so the two layers stick together but not enough for the filling to come out the sides. Top the cheesecake layer with some more whipped cream from the large bowl, and sprinkle evenly with the remaining strawberry pieces. Top with the second cake layer of sponge cake, top side up. Frost the top and sides of the cake with the rest of the whipped cream in the large bowl.

10. To decorate, hull the remaining quart of berries and halve them, from top to tip. Place a ring of berries around the bottom edge of the cake, tip ends up. Using 5 or 6 berry halves, make a star in the center of the cake, pointing the tips of the berries away from the center. Fit a pastry bag with a medium closed-star tip (#35) or medium open-star tip (#32) and fill with the cream from the small bowl. Pipe shells or rosettes (page 26) around the top edge of the cake and make a large rosette on top of the strawberry pieces.

11. Refrigerate the cake until serving time (it takes at least 2 hours to allow the cheesecake to thaw enough to slice easily. Use a sharp straight-edge knife, not a serrated one. Cover any leftover cake and refrigerate. Do not freeze this cake.

7. When the cheesecake and sponge cake are cold and the pastry cream has set, assemble the cake. Keep the cheesecake in the springform and gently spread the pastry cream over it, using a rubber spatula (avoid stirring the cream at this stage, as you might break its gel). Place the sponge cake, top side up, on the pastry cream. Press down gently. Cover the cake (still in the pan) with plastic wrap and freeze overnight.

8. To decorate the top of the cake with the fudge mirror, combine the ice cream topping and corn syrup in a small saucepan over low heat, stirring just until it's spreadable (don't overheat or let boil!). Take the cake out of the freezer and, using a long, narrow metal spatula, quickly spread the fudge over the top while it's still in the pan. Using the tip of a pointed knife, push a few drips over the edge of the cake (in the space between the cake and the inside edge of the pan). This gives the cake a finished look. Return the pan to the freezer until the mirror has set (do not cover), about 30 minutes.

9. Fill a pastry bag fitted with a small round tip (#2) with the whipped cream. Pipe a white web on top of the cake, making thin lines ⅜ inch apart (don't worry if the lines are a little wavy, as that's a nice homemade touch). Return the cake to the freezer until the web has set, about 30 minutes more.

10. To serve, let the cake stand at room temperature for 10 minutes, then release and remove the ring of the springform, leaving the cake on the bottom of the pan. Place on a serving plate and refrigerate until ready to serve (this cake takes about 2 hours in the refrigerator to thaw enough to easily slice). Use a sharp straight-edge knife, not a serrated one, to cut it. Refrigerate any leftover cake or wrap and freeze for up to 1 month.

*Junior's triple-decker carrot cake covered with cream cheese frosting is one of its best-selling desserts. Replace one of the layers with cheesecake and you have another towering winner. "One of the reasons that Junior's carrot cakes taste so great," explains Alan Rosen, "is because we grate fresh carrots for every cake."*

# carrot cake
## cheesecake

**MAKES ONE 9-INCH THREE-LAYER CAKE, ABOUT 5 INCHES HIGH**

1 cheesecake layer, as prepared in Boston Cream Pie Cheesecake (page 154)

**FOR THE CARROT CAKE (3 LAYERS):**

2 cups all-purpose flour

2 teaspoons baking powder

2 teaspoons ground cinnamon

3/4 teaspoon salt

1/2 teaspoon baking soda

1/2 cup dark raisins

Boiling water

4 extra-large eggs

2 cups granulated sugar

1 cup vegetable oil

1/4 cup heavy or whipping cream

1 tablespoon pure vanilla extract

2 cups peeled and finely grated carrots (about 4 large)

3/4 cup peeled, cored, and minced apples (about 2 medium-size)

3/4 cup finely chopped walnuts

*(continued on page 159)*

*1.* Prepare the cheesecake layer in a buttered 9-inch springform pan as directed, then cool in the pan on a wire rack for 2 hours, cover with plastic wrap, and refrigerate until completely cold, about 4 hours. Place in the freezer overnight and/or until ready to assemble the cake.

*2.* Meanwhile, prepare the carrot cake layers. Check that the oven is preheated to 325°F and that the water bath has been removed. Generously butter the bottom and sides of three 9-inch round layer cake pans (you'll need three layers, two for the cake and one to break into crumbs for the top). *Very important:* Line the bottom of all three pans with parchment or waxed paper (don't let the paper come up the sides).

*3.* Sift the flour, baking powder, cinnamon, salt, and baking soda together in a medium-size bowl and set aside. Place the raisins in a small saucepan, cover them with boiling water, cover the pan, and let soak until nice and plump, about 15 to 20 minutes. Drain well and let stand on paper towels.

*4.* Meanwhile, beat the eggs in a large bowl with an electric mixer on high until light yellow, about 5 minutes. With the mixer still running, gradually add the granulated sugar, then slowly drizzle in the oil, then the cream and vanilla. When the batter is light golden and airy, it's ready (this usually takes a total of 15 to 20 minutes of beating). Stir in the flour mixture with a wooden spoon,

**FOR THE CREAM CHEESE FROSTING:**

Three 8-ounce packages cream cheese (use only full fat), at room temperature

1 cup (2 sticks) unsalted butter, at room temperature

6 cups sifted confectioners' sugar (1½ pounds)

1 tablespoon pure vanilla extract

¼ cup heavy or whipping cream

*The Junior's Way*

Be sure to grate the carrots very fine for this cake. If you have a food processor with a fine grating disk, use it. If not, use the small holes on a hand grater.

then stir in the carrots, apples, walnuts, and raisins. Divide the batter evenly between the three cake pans and bake until the centers spring back when lightly touched and a toothpick inserted in the centers comes out with moist crumbs, about 45 minutes. Let the cakes cool in the pans on a wire rack for 15 minutes, then turn them out onto the rack and peel off the paper liners. Let the cakes cool completely, about 2 hours, then wrap each layer in plastic wrap and refrigerate.

*5.* When you're ready to assemble the cake, remove the frozen cheesecake from the freezer and let stand at room temperature for 10 minutes while you make the frosting. Beat the cream cheese and butter together in a medium-size bowl with the mixer on high speed. Add the confectioners' sugar, then the vanilla, beating until smooth. With the mixer running, gradually add the cream and beat until the frosting looks whipped and creamy. Add a little more cream if necessary until it's easy to spread. Set out the carrot cake layers and break the least attractive one into coarse crumbs.

*6.* To assemble, place one of the remaining two cake layers on a cake plate, top side down. Spread with some of the frosting. Release and remove the ring of the springform, then remove the frozen cheesecake from the bottom of the pan (see Solution, page 14). Place the cheesecake, top side down, on top of the frosted carrot cake layer and spread with some frosting. Top with the remaining cake layer, top side up. Ice the top and sides of the cake with the remaining frosting. Decorate the top edge of the cake with a ring of cake crumbs about 2 inches wide. Refrigerate the cake until ready to serve (it takes this cake about 2 hours in the refrigerator to thaw enough to easily slice). Use a sharp straight-edge knife, not a serrated one, to cut it. If there's any cake leftover, cover it and refrigerate, or wrap and freeze for up to 1 month.

ter of the cake). Place the sponge cake, top side down, on a cake plate. Spread with a thin layer of whipped cream from the large bowl, sprinkle with about ⅔ cup of the coconut, and gently spread with half of the lemon custard. Release and remove the ring of the springform, then remove the frozen cheesecake from the bottom of the pan (see Solution, page 14). Place top side down on the custard. Top the cheesecake with some more whipped cream, sprinkle with about ⅔ cup coconut, and spread with the remaining custard in the large bowl.

7. To decorate, frost the top and sides of the cake with the remaining whipped cream in the large bowl. Using your fingers, gently pat coconut on the side of the cake and sprinkle the rest on top. Fit a pastry bag with a medium closed-star tip (#35) or medium open-star tip (#32) and fill with the cream from the small bowl. Pipe shells or rosettes (see page 26) around the top edge of the cake and a circle of 7 whipped cream rosettes in the center. Fill the circle with the 2 tablespoons reserved lemon custard.

8. Refrigerate the cake for at least 2 hours to allow the cheesecake to thaw enough to slice easily). Use a sharp straight-edge knife, not a serrated one, to cut it. Cover any leftover cake with plastic wrap and refrigerate, or wrap and freeze for up to 1 month.

## The Junior's Way

Master Baker Michael Goodman advises: "Work fast when assembling this cake and be sure to keep the lemon filling and the whipped cream that you're not using chilled in the refrigerator. It's important to have both of these as cold as possible when 'building' this cake."

*One day Alan's dad, Walter said, "Why not make a plain cheesecake cake and put it inside a devil's food cake?" That's how this popular cake began! It measures over five inches tall, with three layers of devil's food cake and one of cheesecake—plus plenty of rich, fudgy frosting to hold it all together. This is a guaranteed show stopper for any occasion.*

# devil's food cheesecake

**MAKES ONE 9-INCH FOUR-LAYER CAKE, ABOUT 5 INCHES HIGH**

1 cheesecake layer as prepared
in Boston Cream Pie Cheesecake
(page 154)

**FOR THE DEVIL'S FOOD CAKE
(3 LAYERS):**

2¼ cups sifted cake flour

2 teaspoons baking powder

½ teaspoon salt

¾ cup (1½ sticks) unsalted butter,
at room temperature

1 cup granulated sugar

½ cup firmly packed
dark brown sugar

3 extra-large eggs, separated

4 ounces bittersweet
or semisweet chocolate, melted
(page 23) and cooled

1 tablespoons pure vanilla extract

1½ cups milk (use whole, not 2%
or skim)

½ teaspoon cream of tartar

*(continued on page 168)*

*1.* Prepare the cheesecake layer in a buttered 9-inch springform pan as directed, then cool in the pan on a wire rack for 2 hours, cover with plastic wrap, and refrigerate until completely cold, about 4 hours. Place in the freezer overnight and/or until ready to assemble the cake.

*2.* Meanwhile, prepare the devil's food cake layers. Check that the oven is preheated to 350°F and that the water bath has been removed. Generously butter the bottom and sides of three 9-inch round layer cake pans. *Very important:* Line the bottom of all three pans with parchment or waxed paper (don't let the paper come up the sides).

*3.* Sift the flour, baking powder, and salt together in a small bowl. Cream the butter and both sugars together in a large bowl with the mixer on medium until light yellow and creamy. Add the egg yolks, one at a time, beating well after each. Beat in the melted chocolate and vanilla. Using a wooden spoon, stir in the flour mixture, alternately with the milk, mixing well after each until blended.

*4.* Put the egg whites and cream of tartar in a clean medium-size bowl and beat with clean, dry beaters on high until stiff (but not dry) peaks form. Fold about one-third of the whites into the chocolate batter until they disappear, then gently fold in the remaining whites. Don't worry if you still see a few white specks—they'll disappear during baking. Divide the batter evenly between the three pans. Bake until a toothpick inserted in the centers comes out with moist crumbs clinging to it, about 30 minutes. Cool the cakes in the pans on a rack for 15 minutes, then remove the cakes from the pans and gently peel off the paper liners. Let cool completely, about 2 hours, then cover with plastic wrap and refrigerate overnight or until ready to assemble the cake.

*5.* Early on the day you plan to serve the cake, make the chocolate curls and lay them out on the marble or baking sheet to dry. Now make the frosting: In a large bowl, sift the confectioners' sugar, cocoa, and salt together. In another large bowl, cream the butter with a mixer on high until light yellow and slightly thickened, about 3 minutes. With the mixer still running, beat in the chocolate, corn syrup, and vanilla. Reduce the mixer speed to low and beat in the sugar-cocoa mixture in two additions, beating well after each. Blend in the cream until the frosting is a spreading consistency, adding a little more cream if needed. Whip the frosting on high until light and creamy, about 2 minutes more.

*6.* To assemble the cake, remove the cheesecake from the freezer and let stand at room temperature about 10 minutes. Place one layer of devil's food cake, top side down, on a cake plate and spread with some of the frosting. Release and remove the ring of the springform, then remove the frozen cheesecake from the bottom of the pan (see Solution, page 14). Place top side down on the frosted cake layer and spread with some frosting. Top with the second devil's food layer, top side down. Spread with more frosting and cover with the third devil's food layer, top side up. Brush away any crumbs from the sides and top of the fudge cake layers. Frost the sides and top of the cake with the remaining frosting, spreading the top with frosting about ½ inch deep. Use a long metal spatula that has been warmed under hot running water to smooth out the frosting on the sides and top of the cake. Coat the sides with the chocolate curls, placing them where you want. With a small spatula or table knife, swirl the frosting on top into a decorative design. Or, if you wish, decorate with a crosshatch design: Make about 6 vertical lines, 1 inch apart, then crisscross 6 more horizontal lines the same distance, swirling the icing a little as you go.

*7.* Refrigerate the cake for at least 2 hours to allow the cheesecake to thaw enough to easily slice). Use a sharp straight-edge knife, not a serrated one, to cut it. Cover any leftover cake with plastic wrap and refrigerate, or wrap and freeze for up to 1 month.

**FOR THE CHOCOLATE CURLS:**
12 ounces bittersweet or semisweet chocolate, shaved into large Chocolate Curls (page 21)

**FOR THE DARK FUDGE FROSTING:**
6 cups sifted confectioners' sugar (1½ pounds)
½ cup unsweetened cocoa powder
½ teaspoon salt
1½ cups (3 sticks) unsalted butter, at room temperature
6 ounces bittersweet or semisweet chocolate, melted (page 23) and cooled
2 tablespoons dark corn syrup
2 tablespoons pure vanilla extract
½ cup heavy or whipping cream

# Index